THE PICTURE BOOK OF

KIDS AND ANIMALS

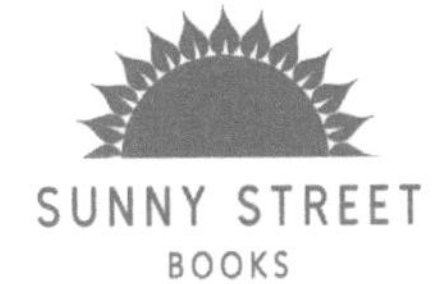

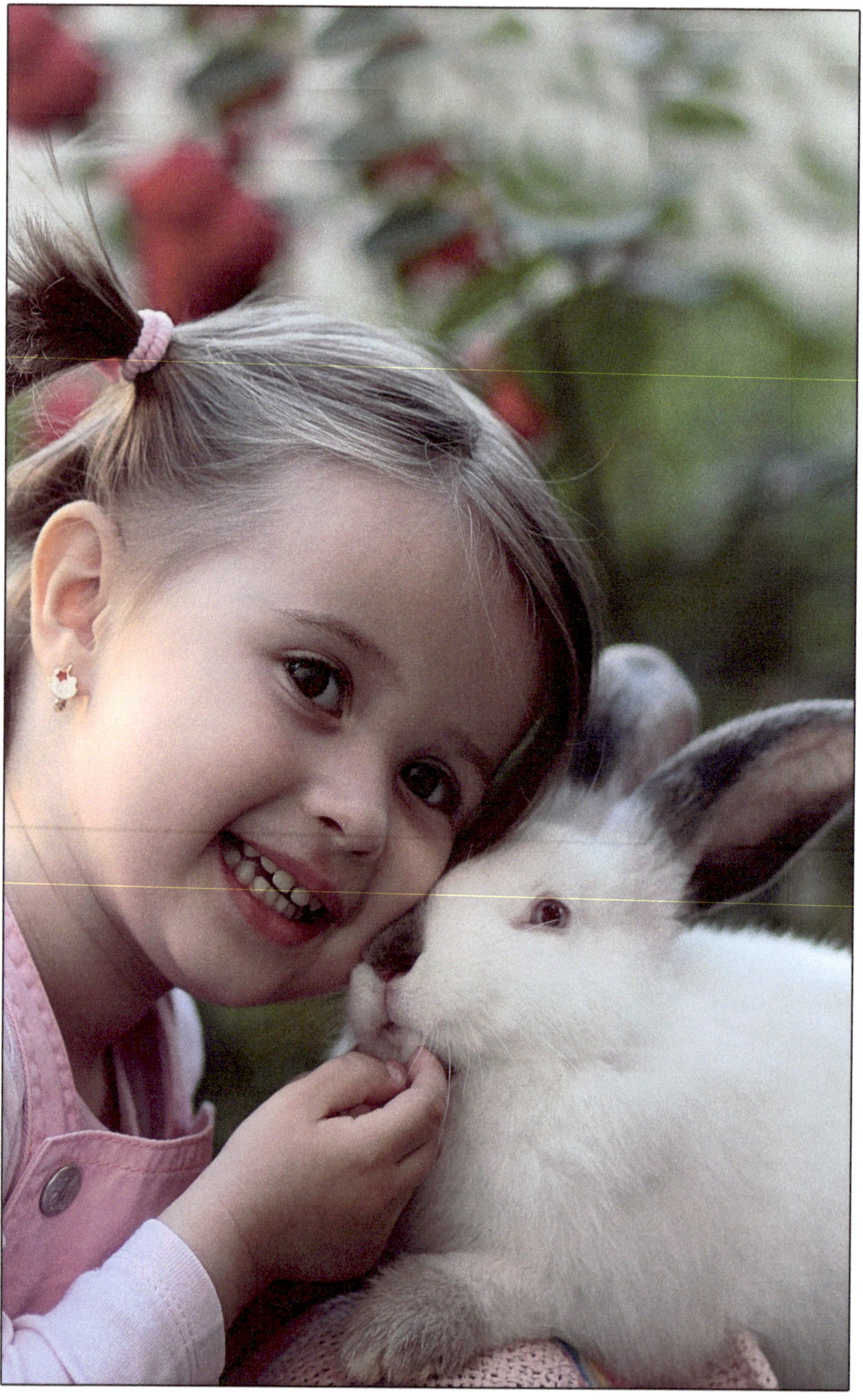

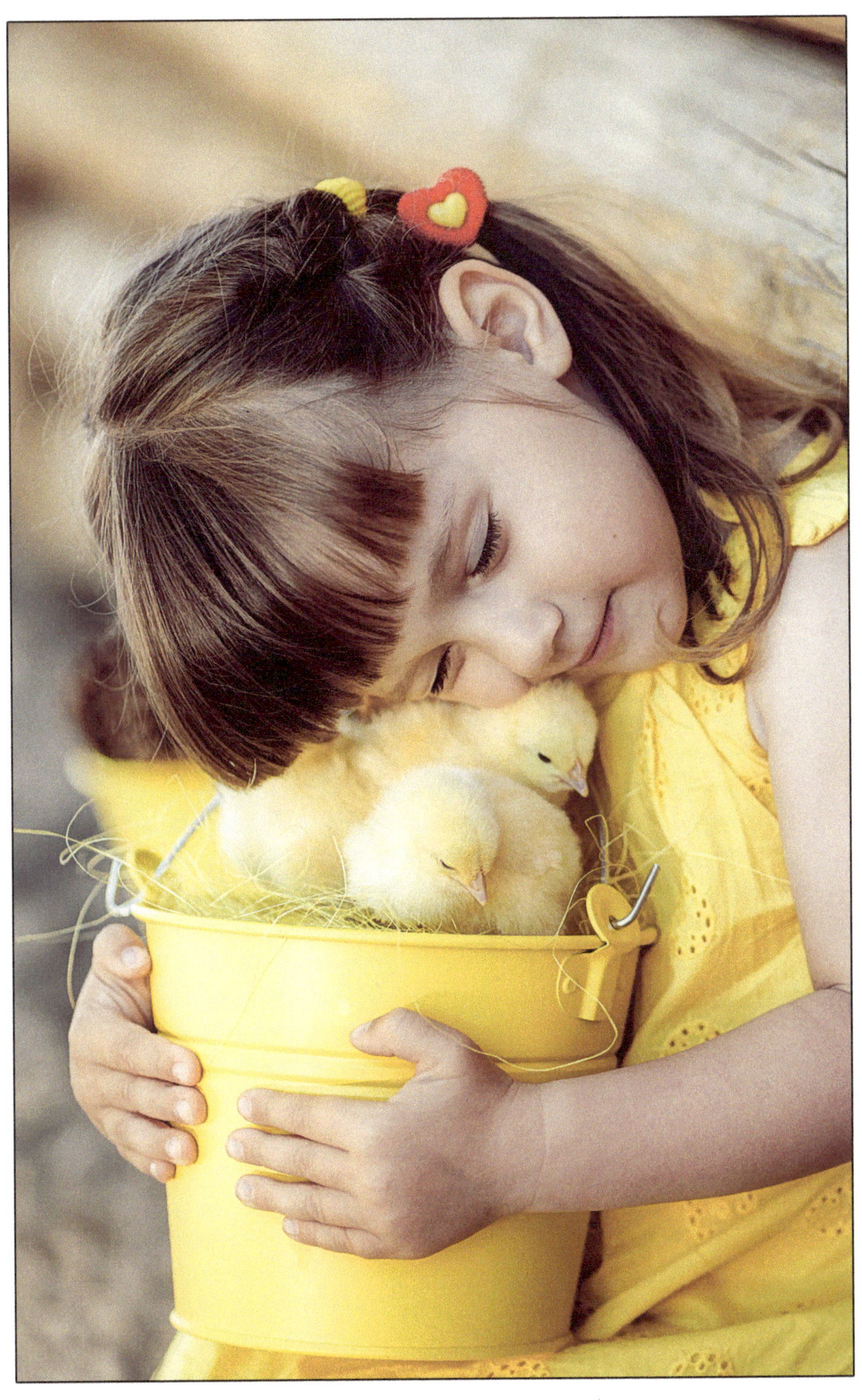

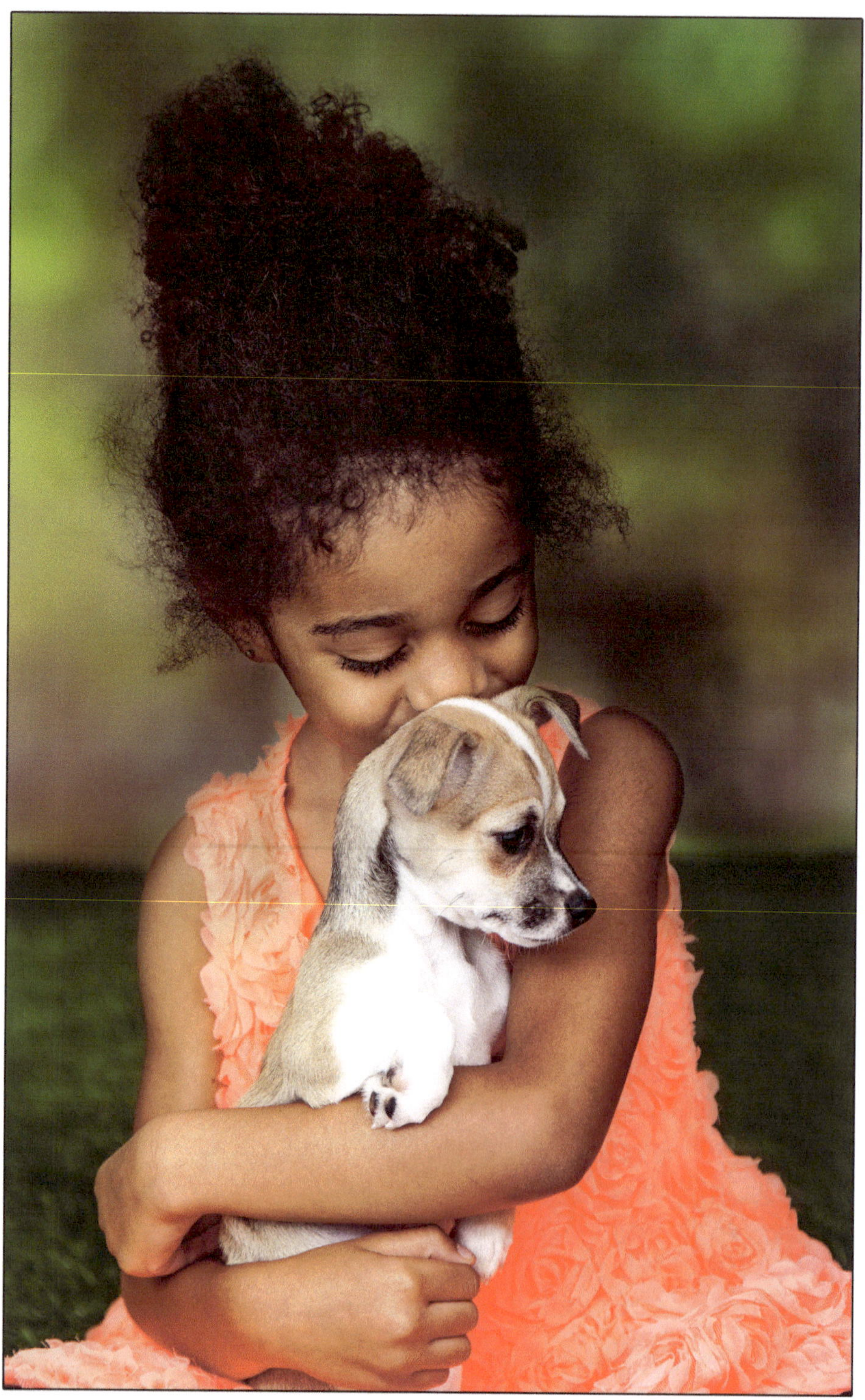

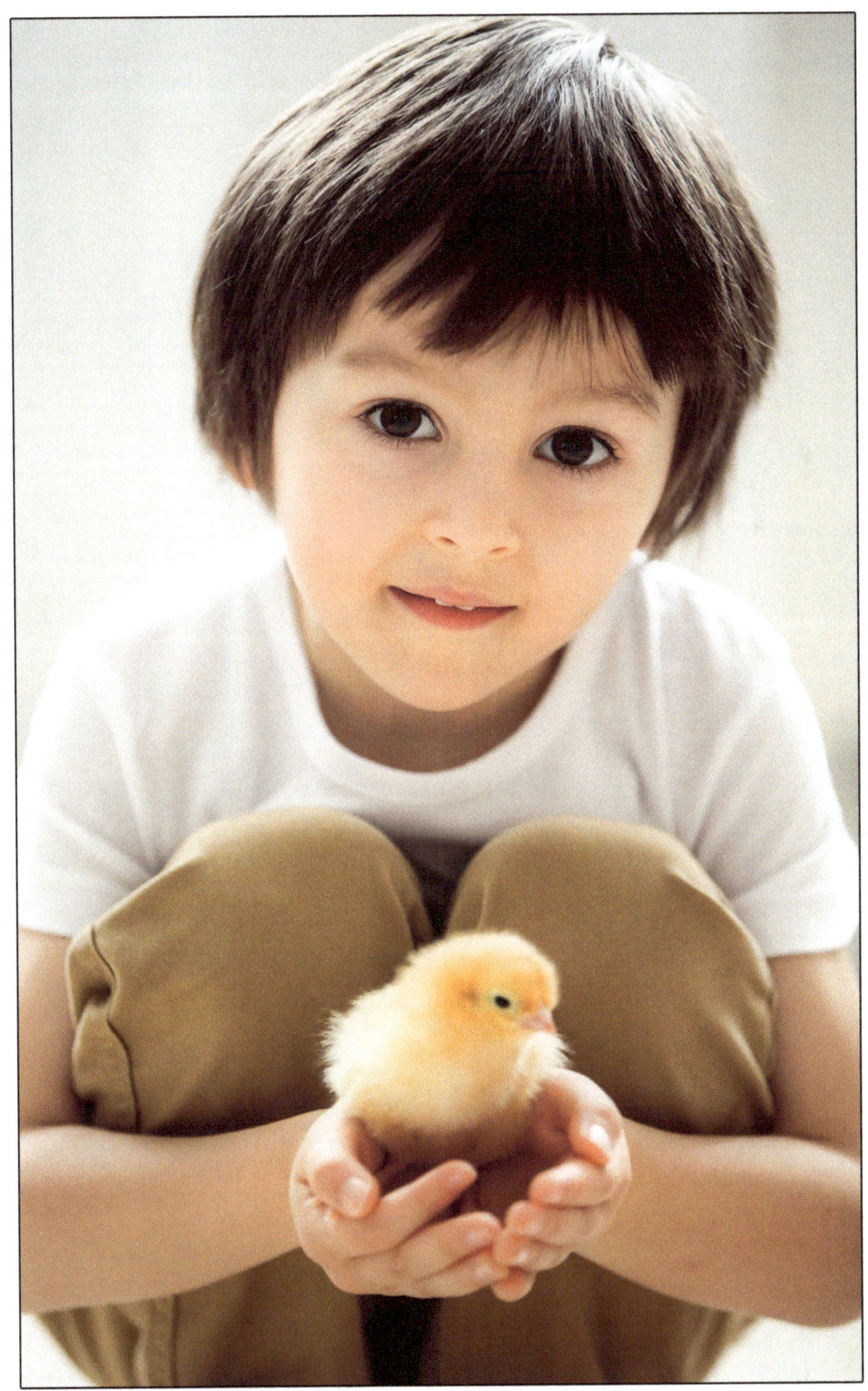

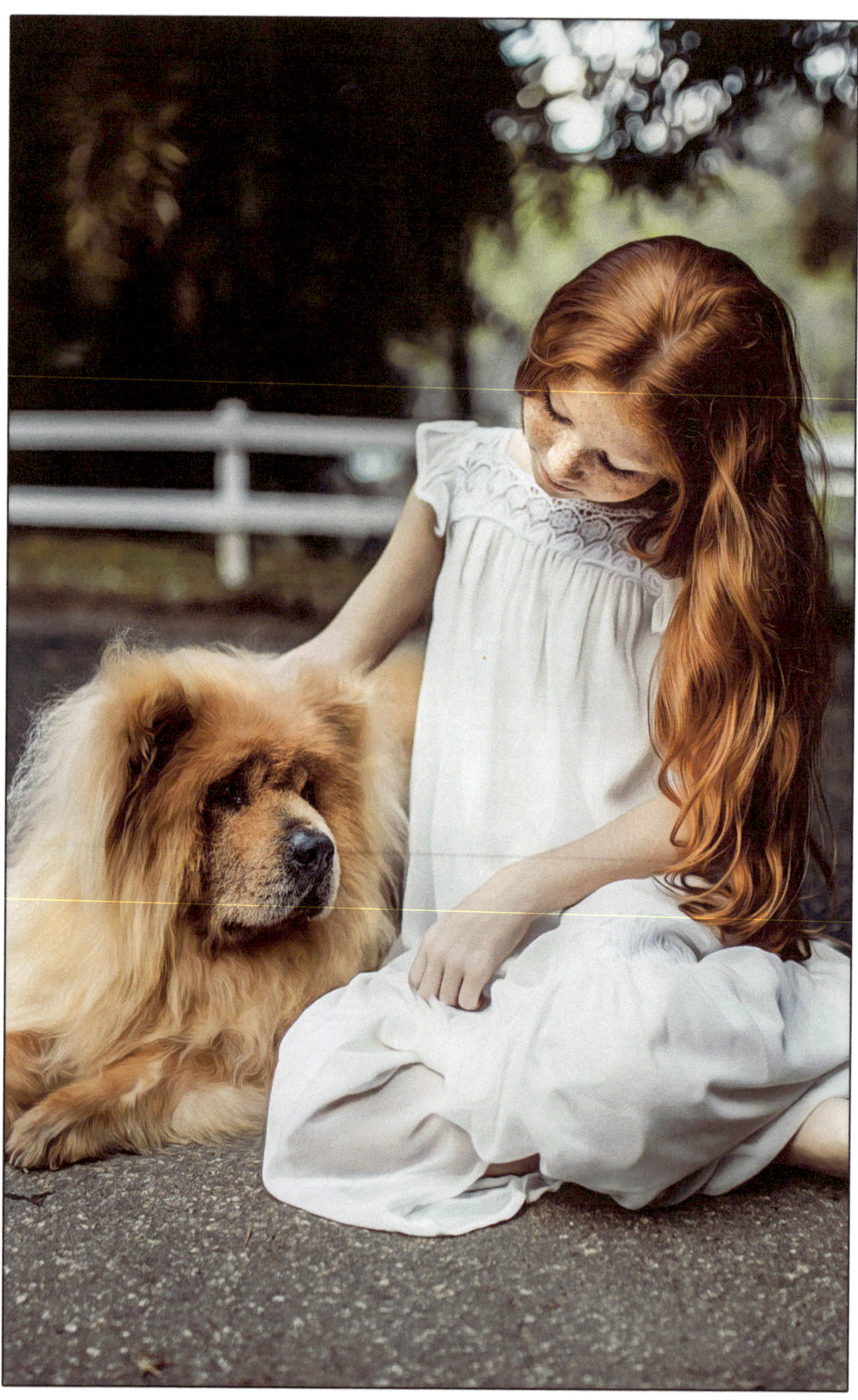

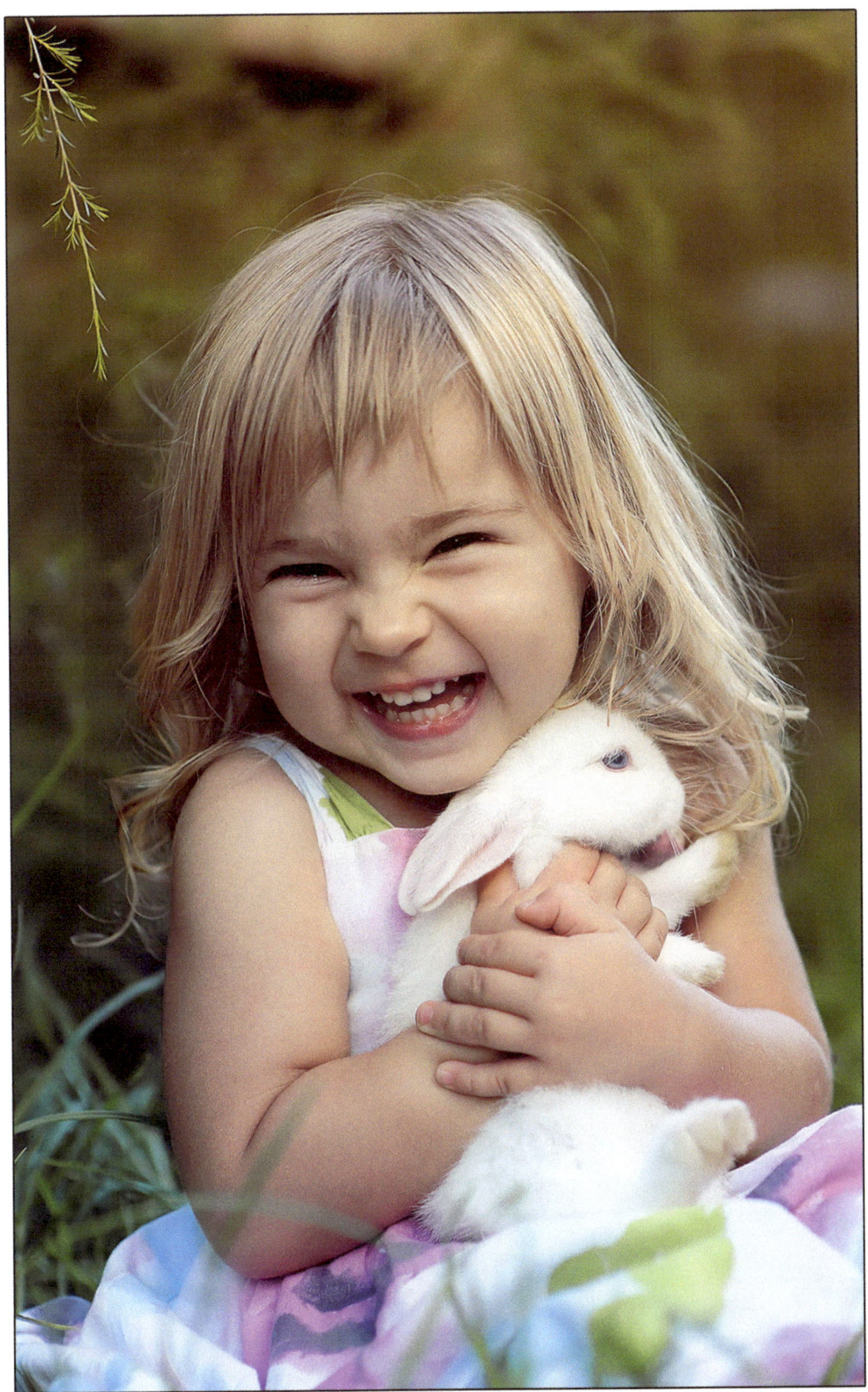

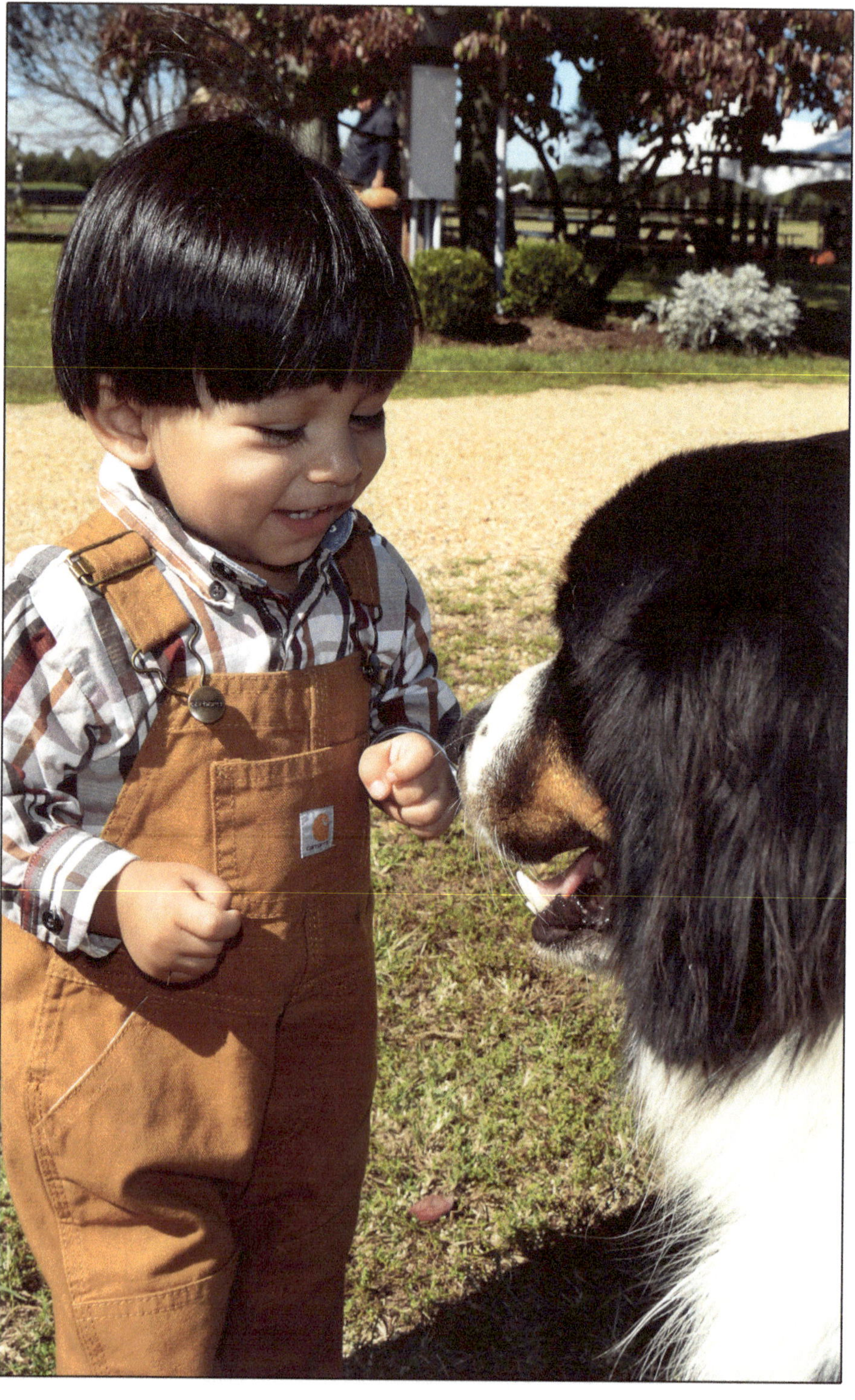

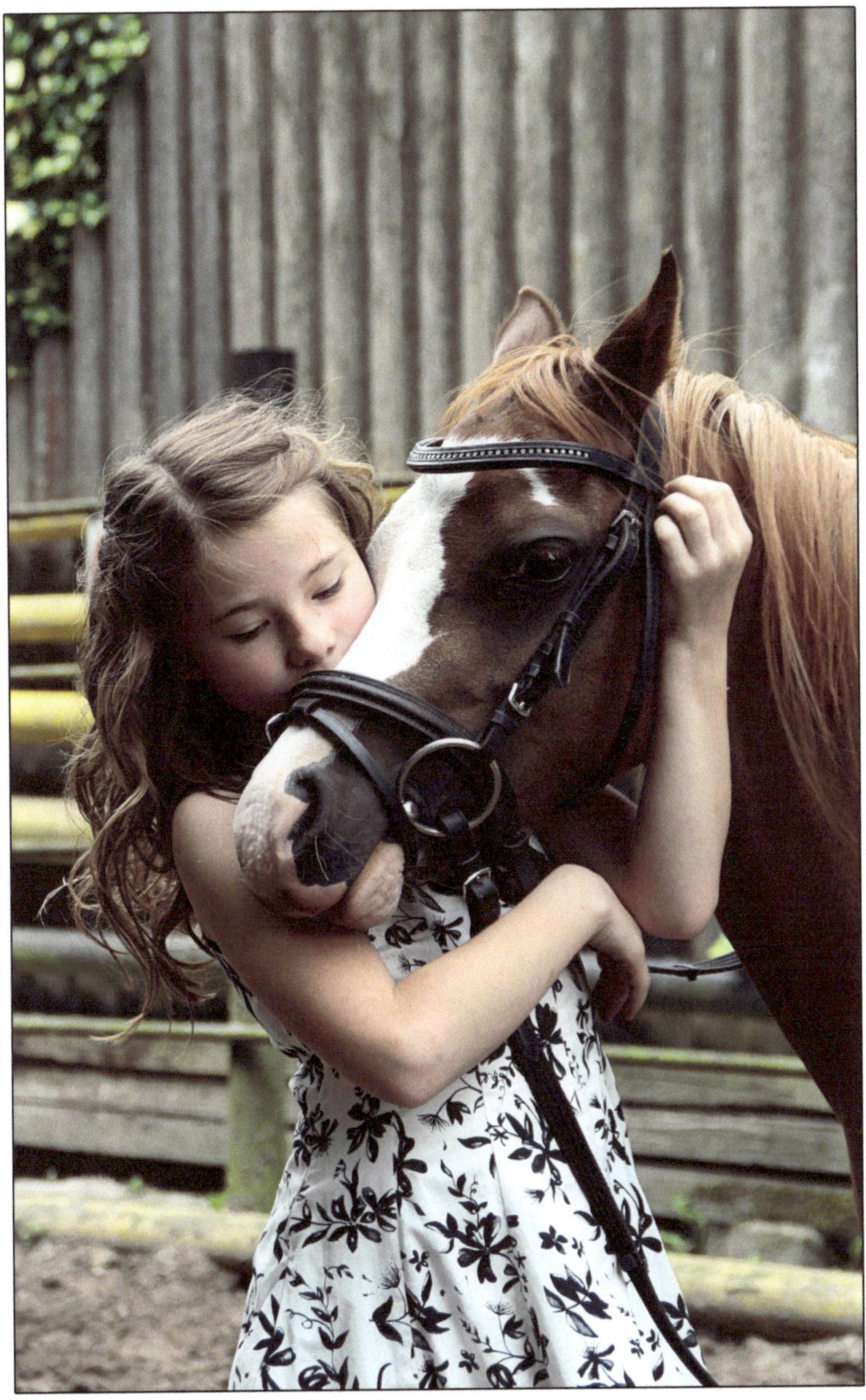

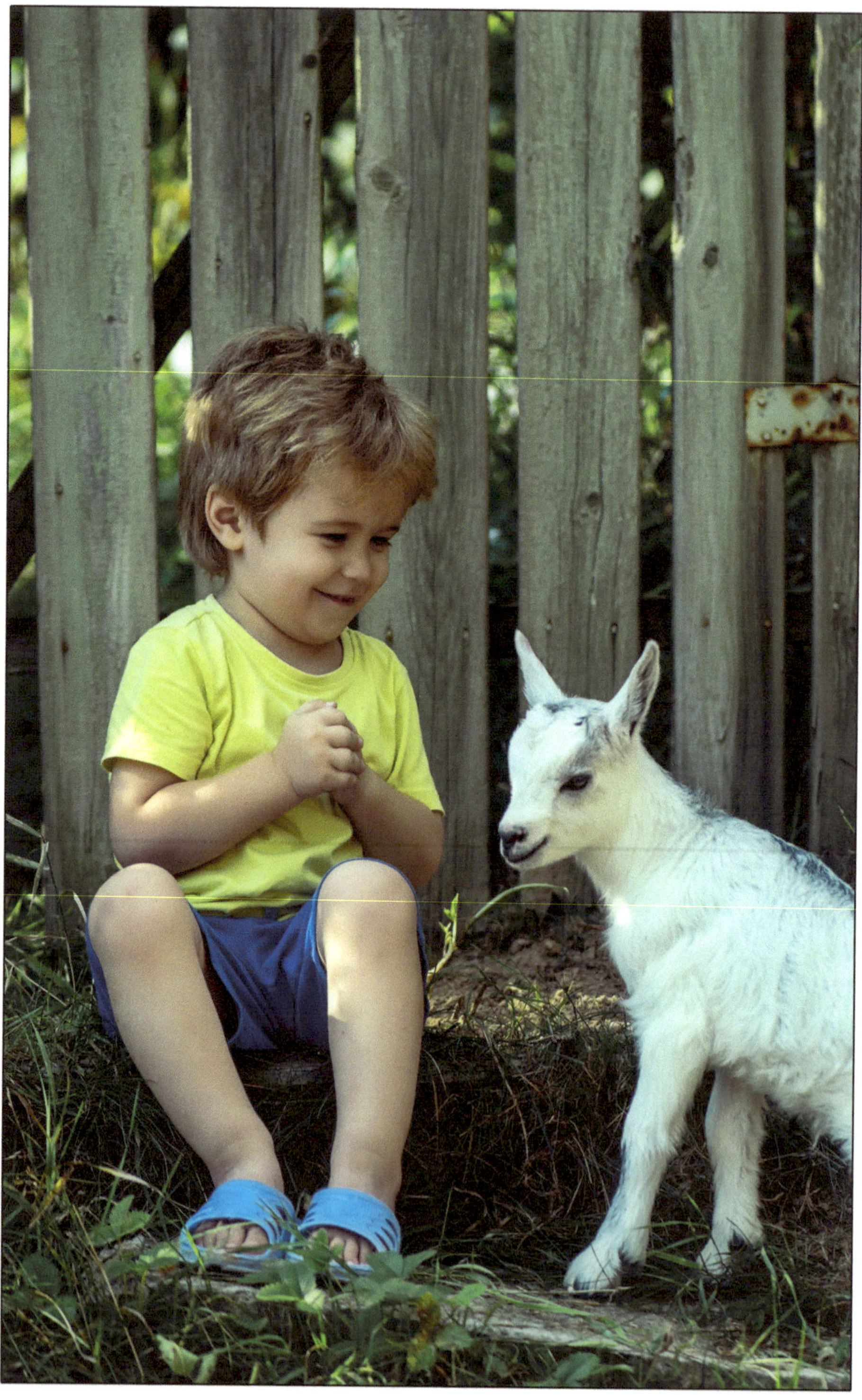

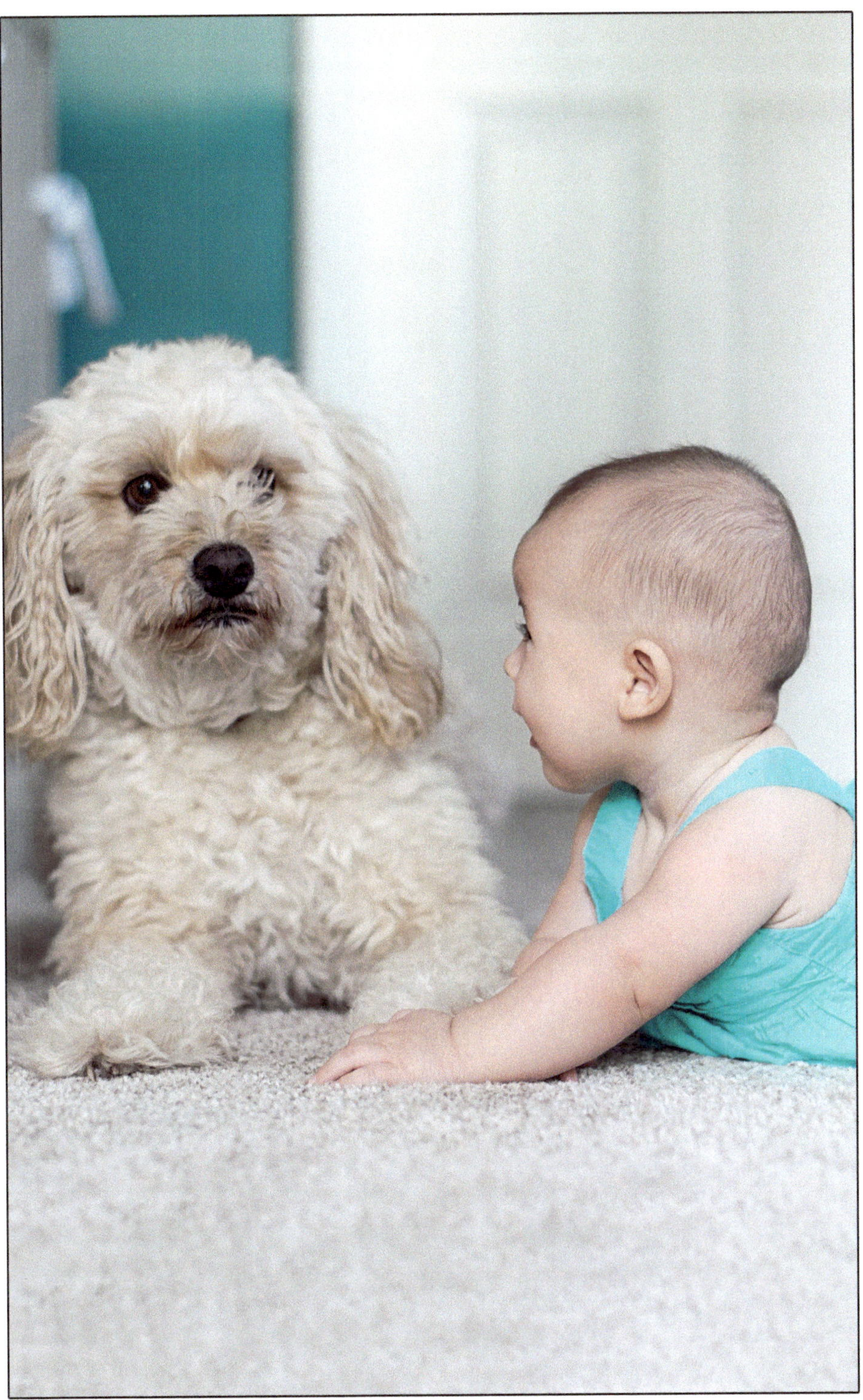

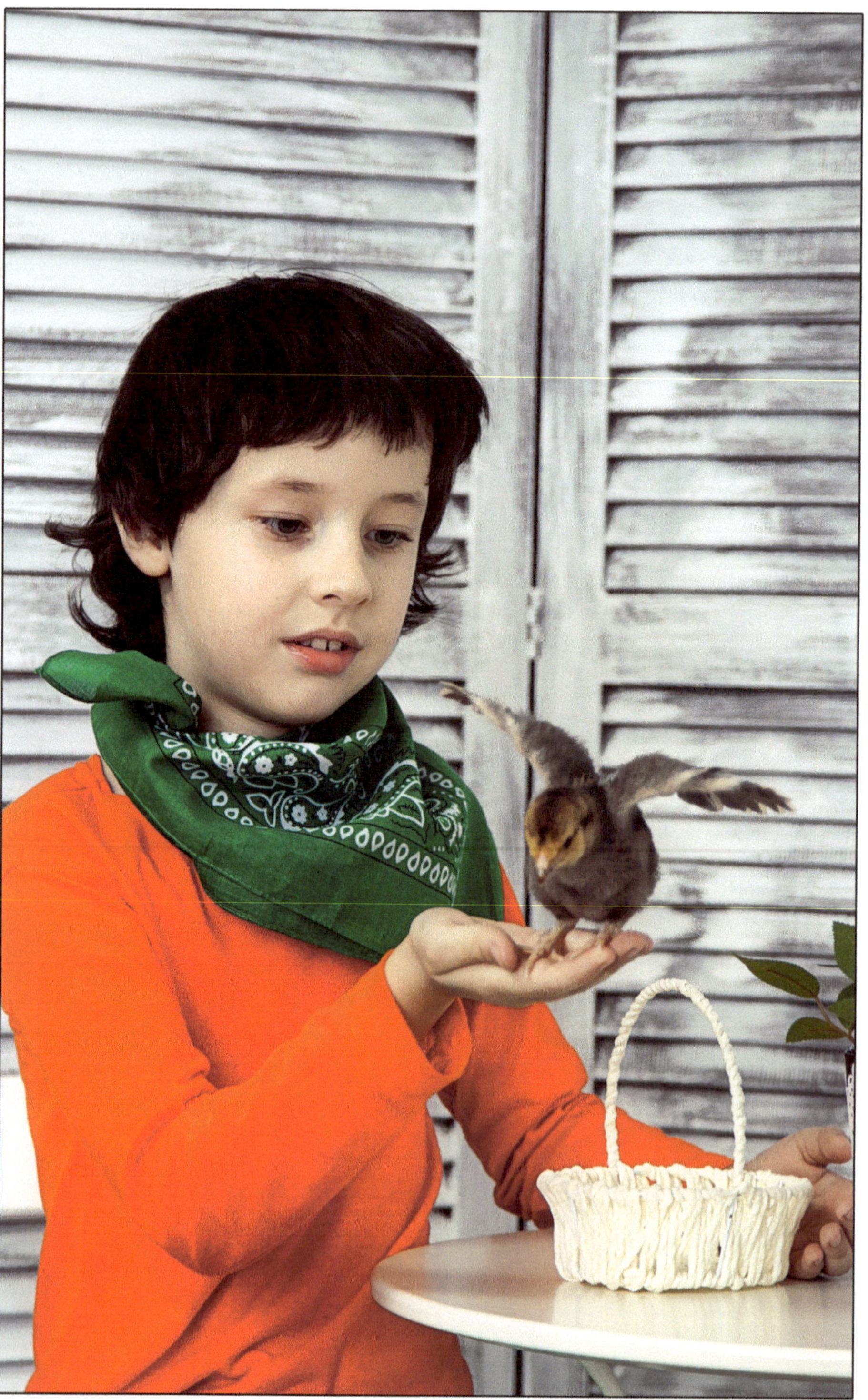

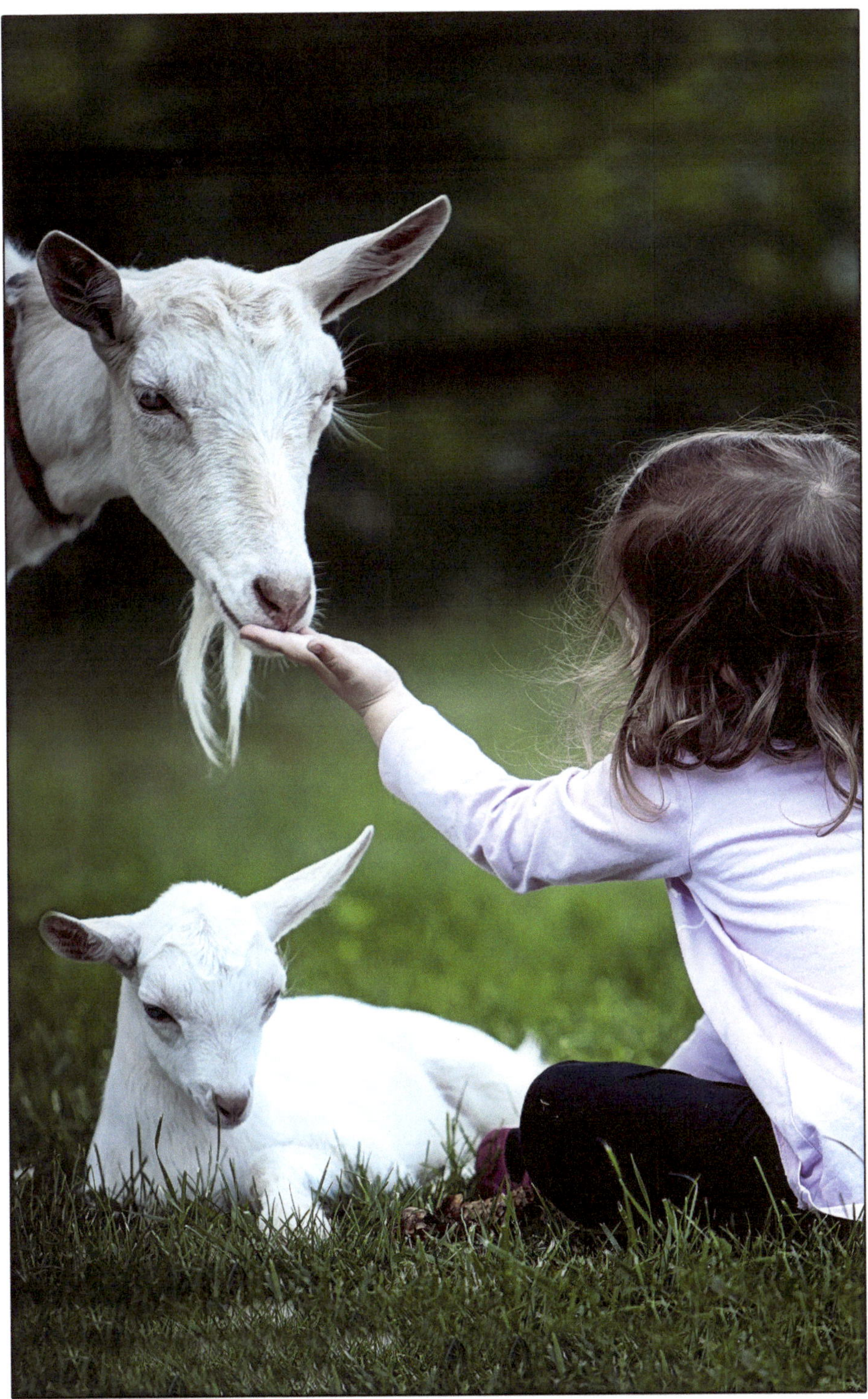

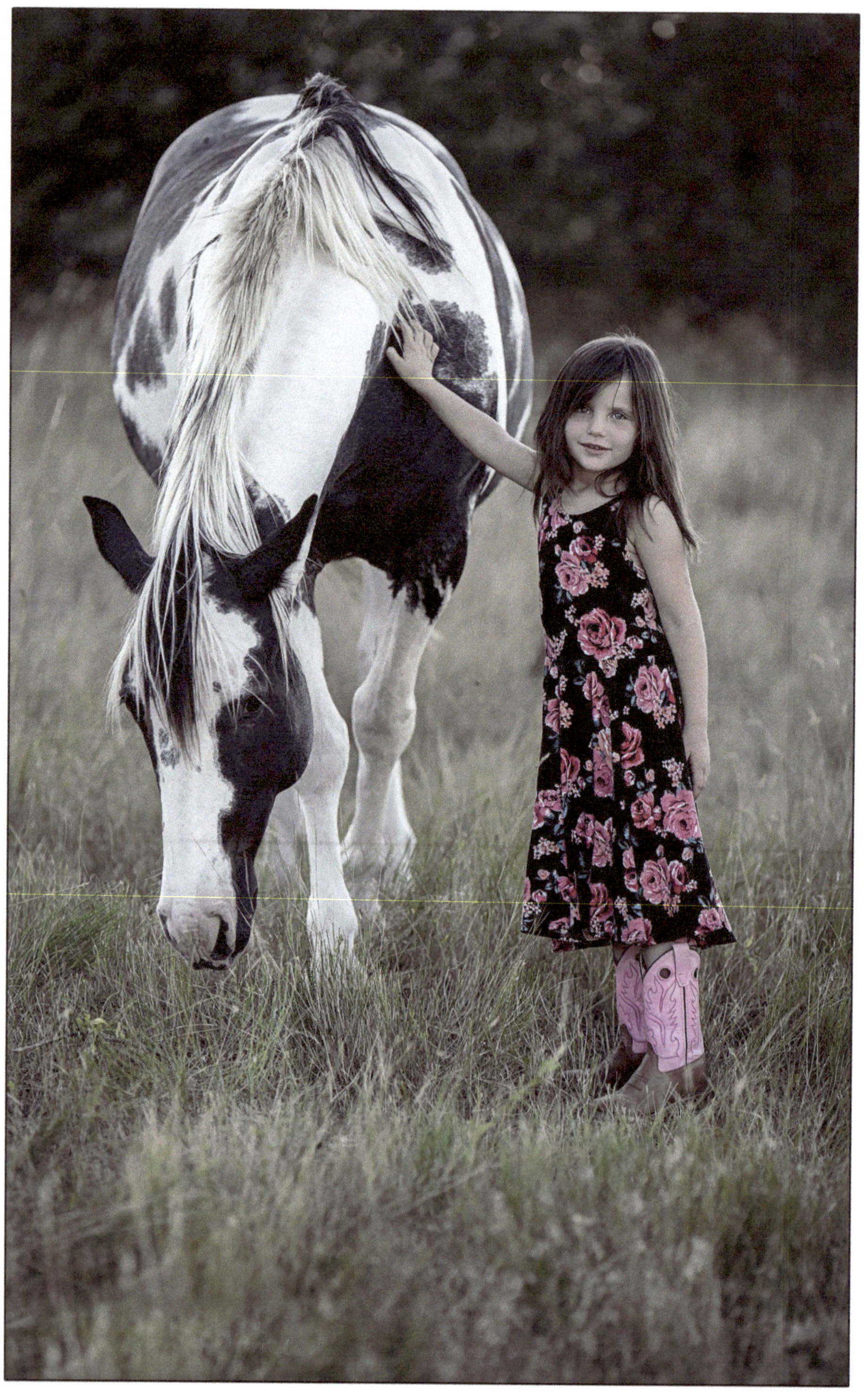

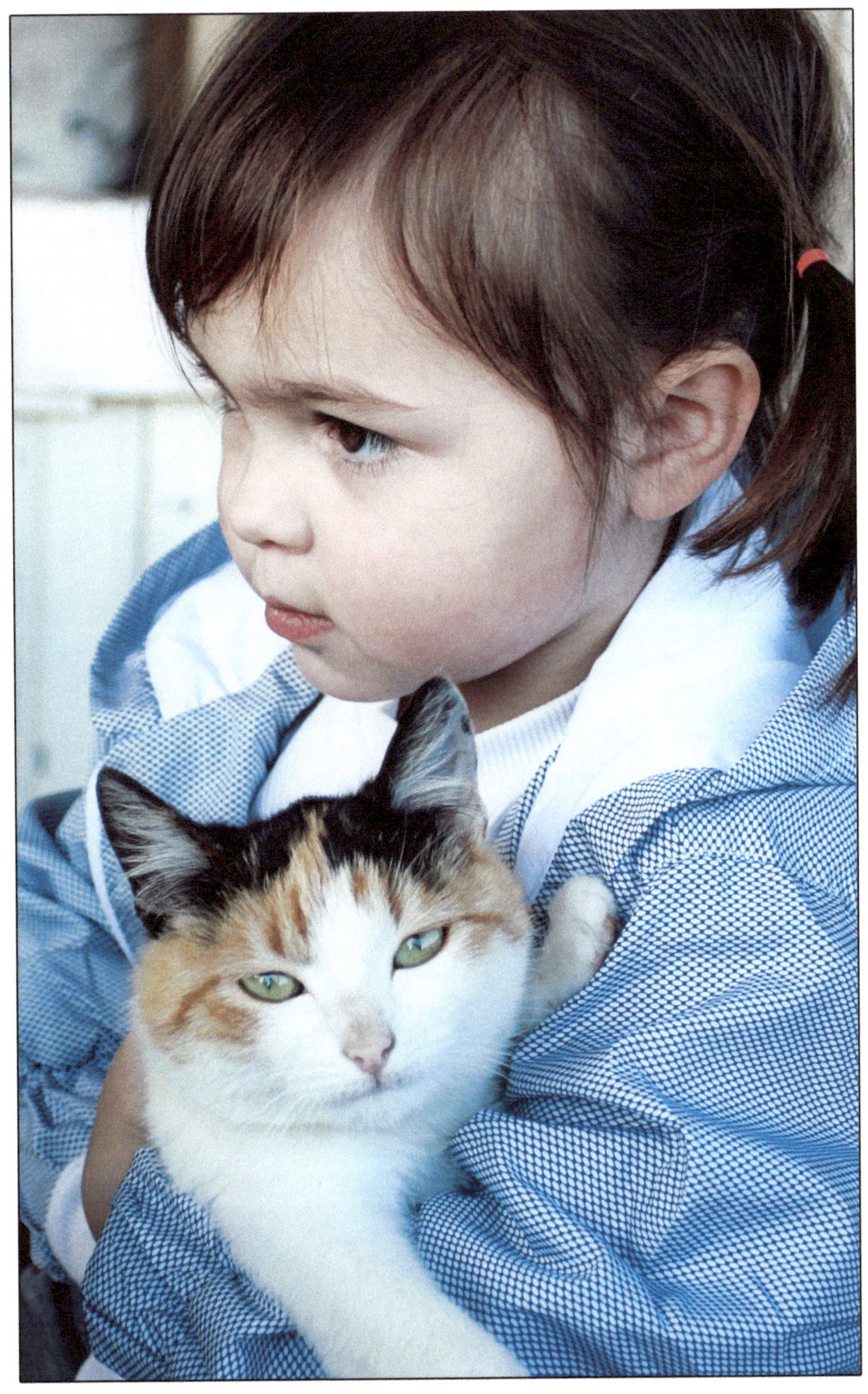

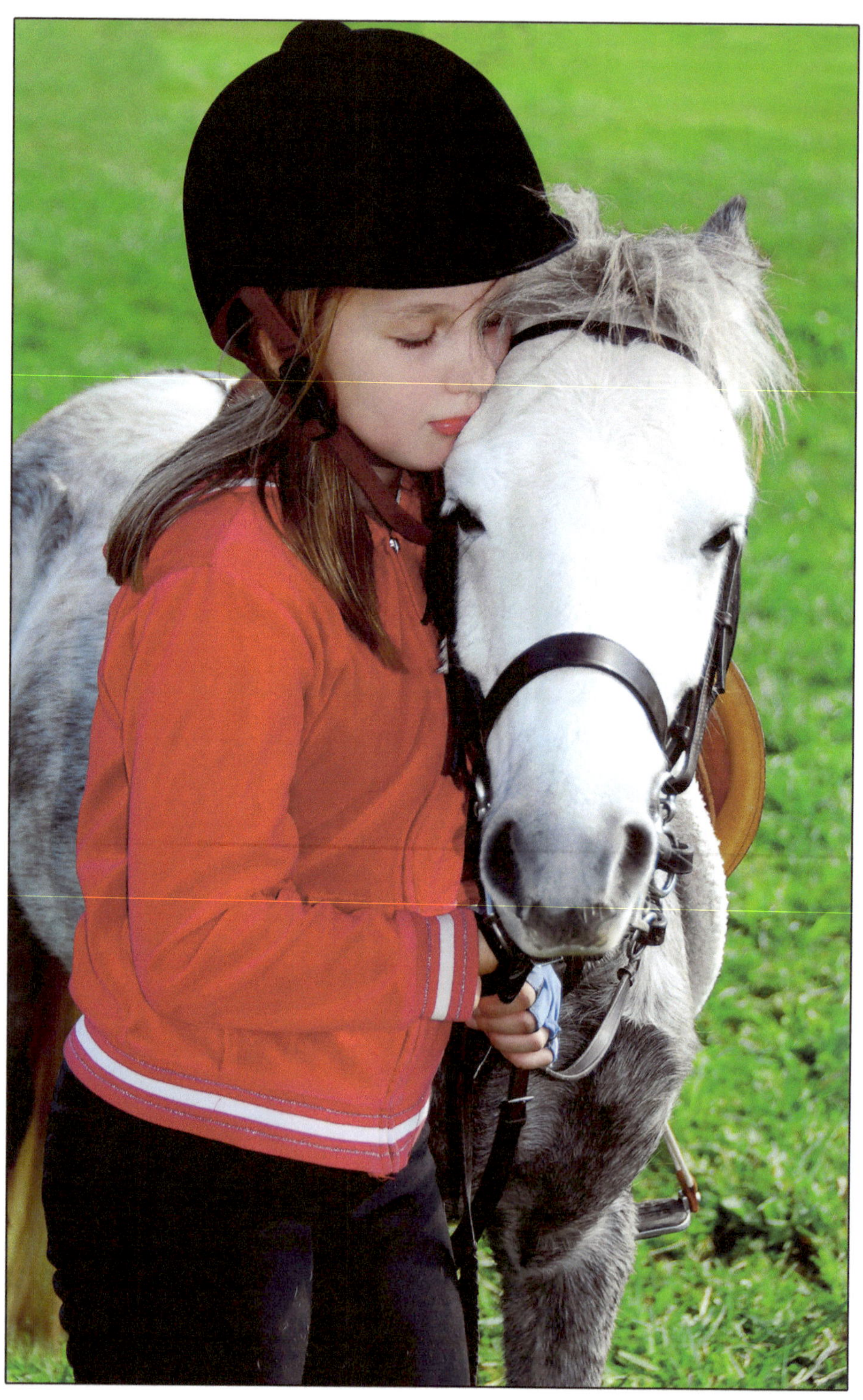

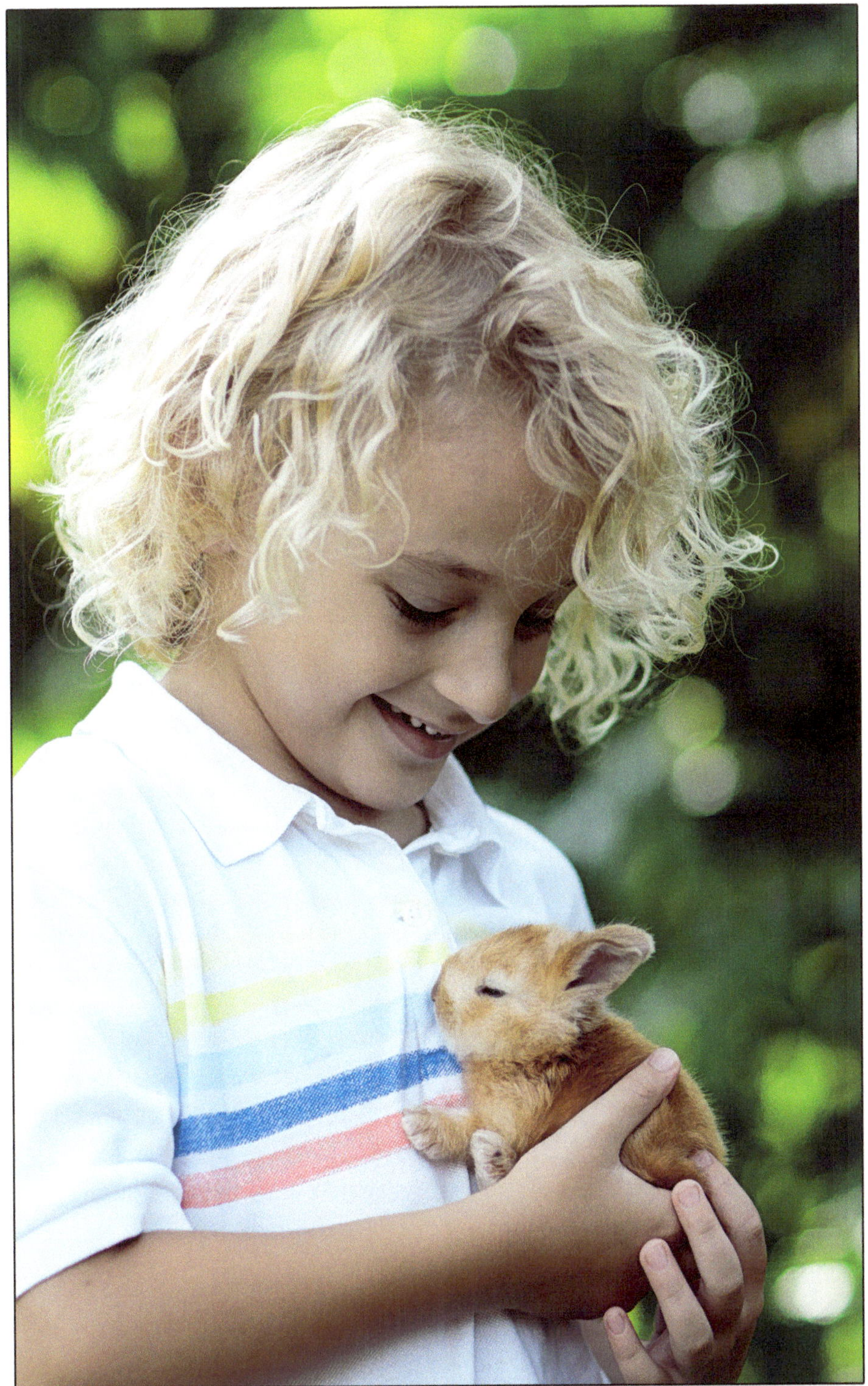

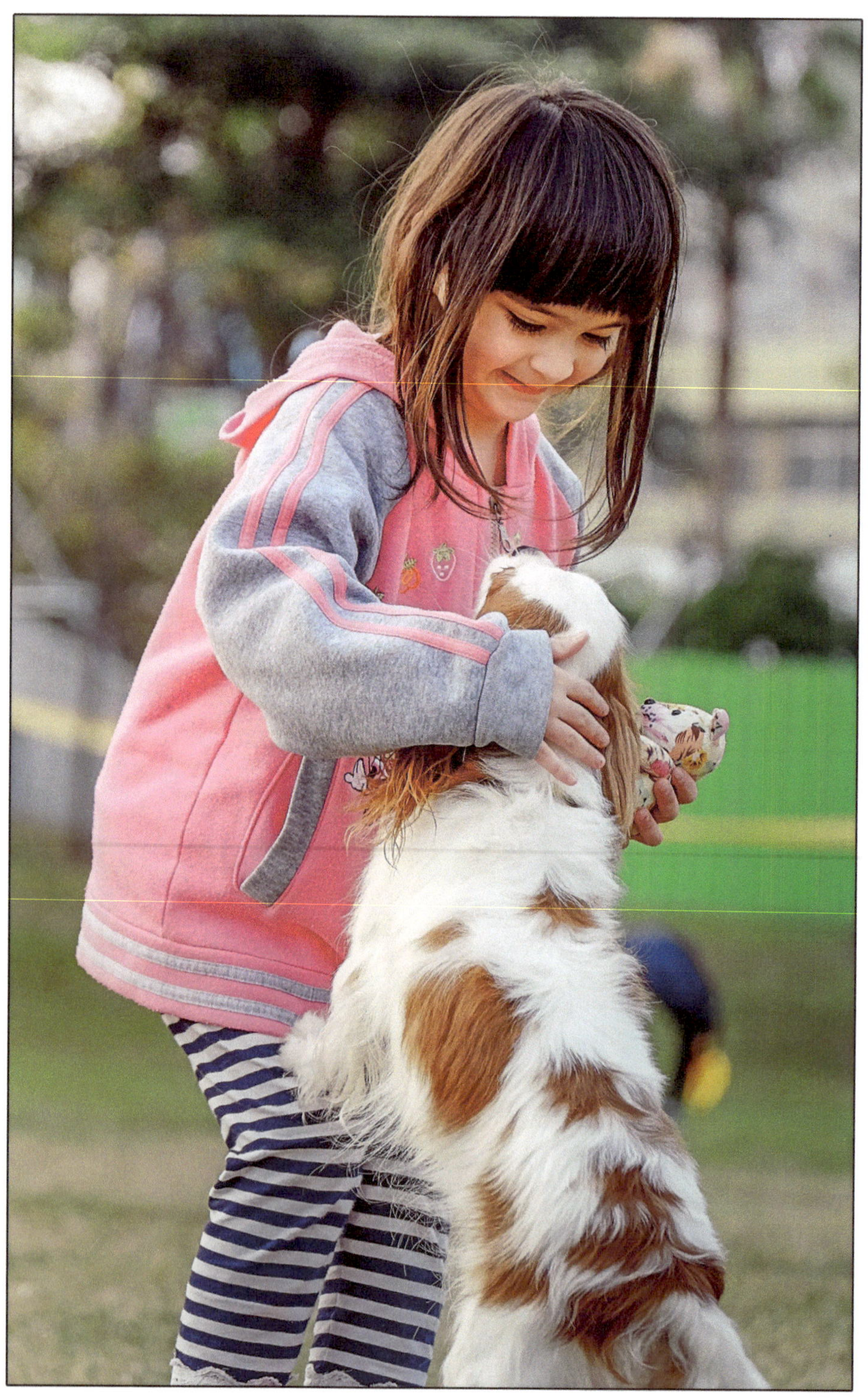

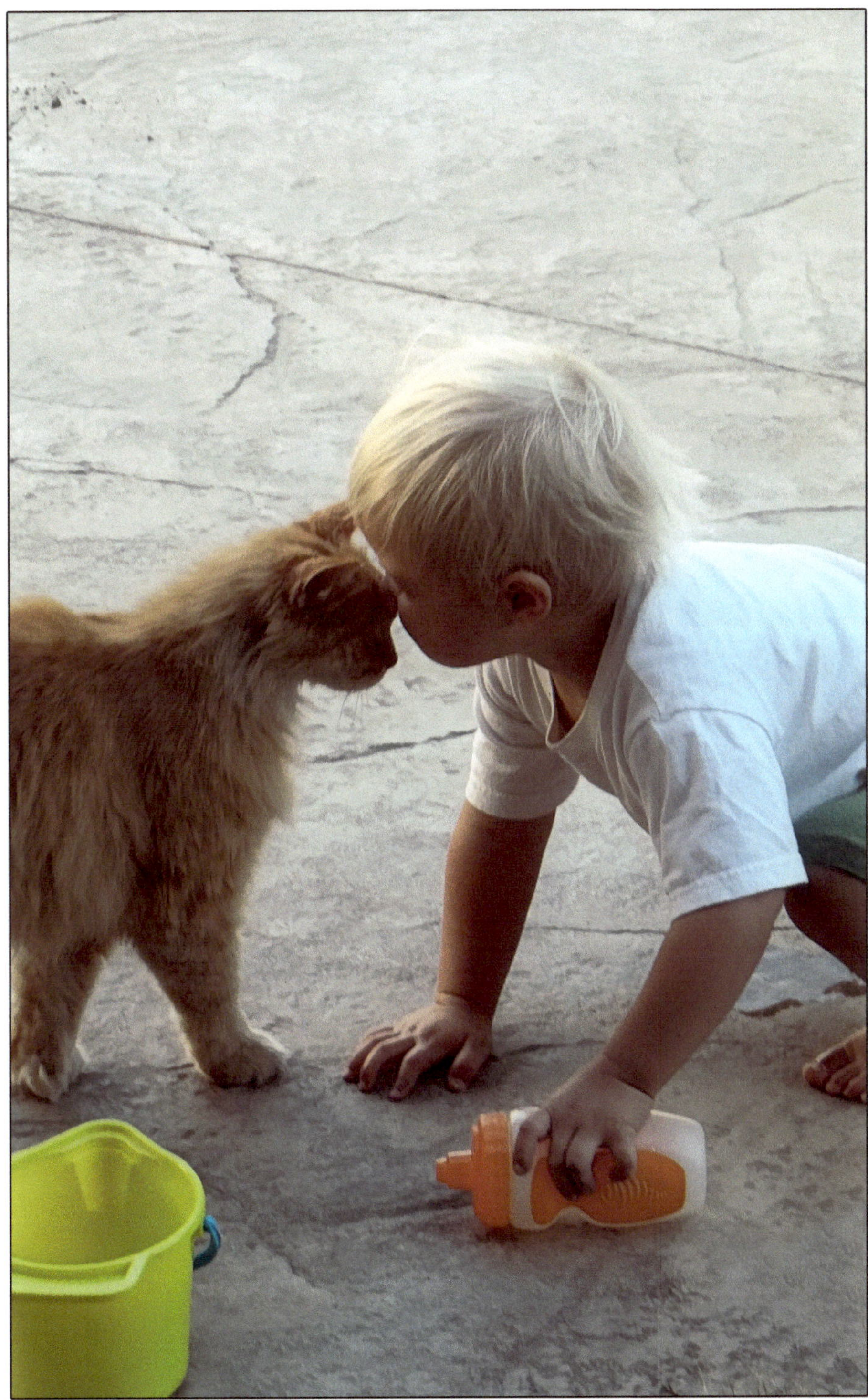

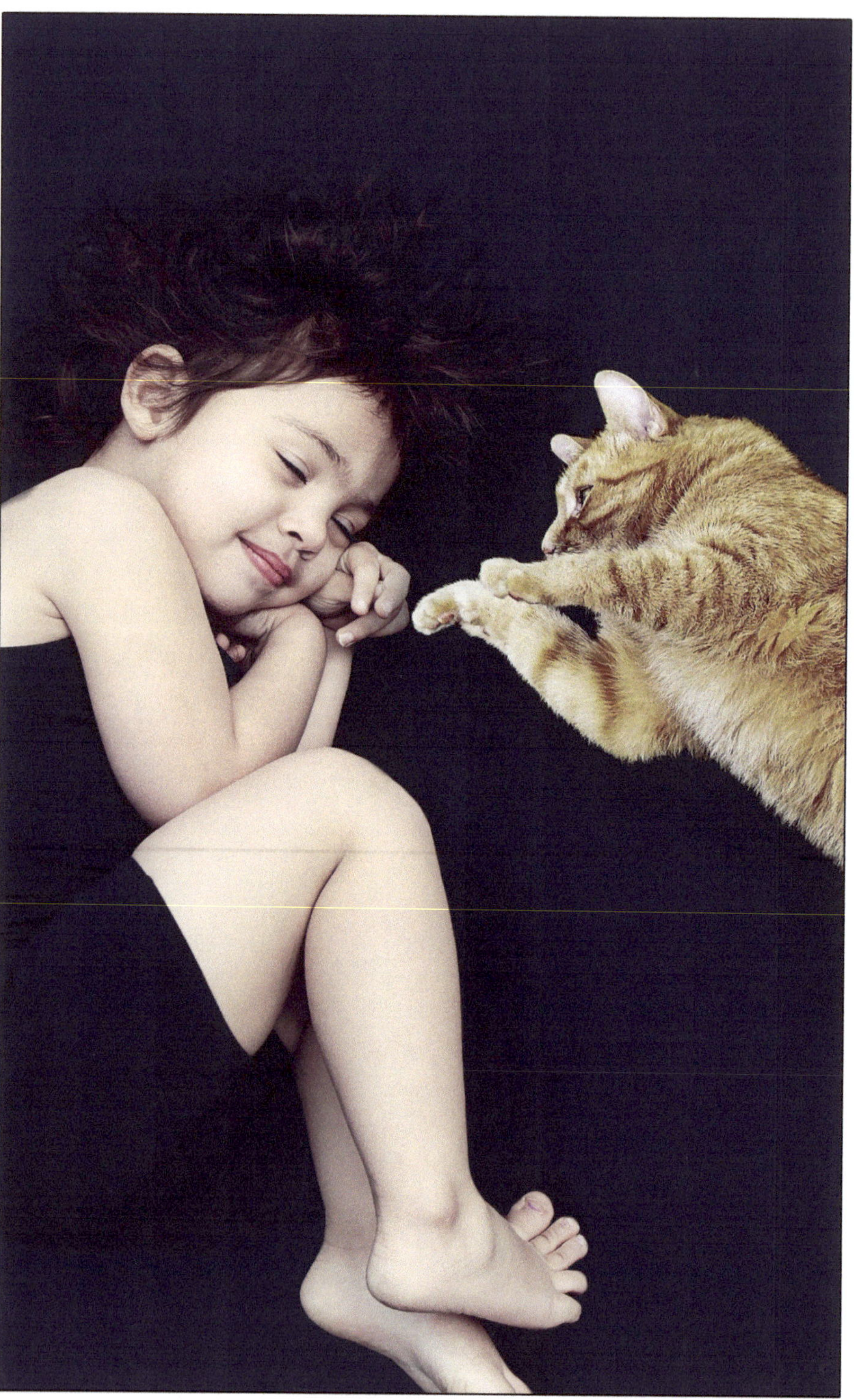

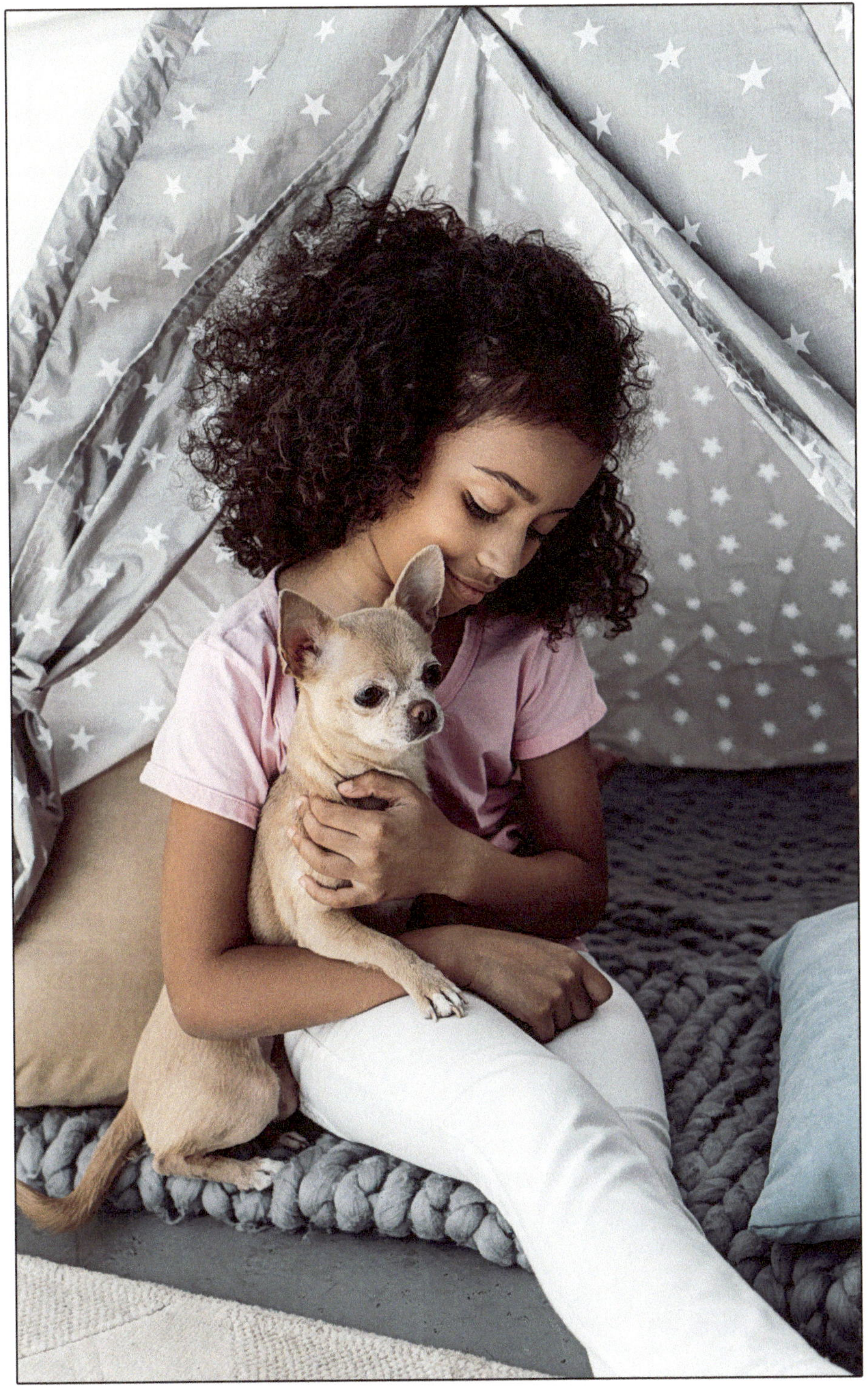

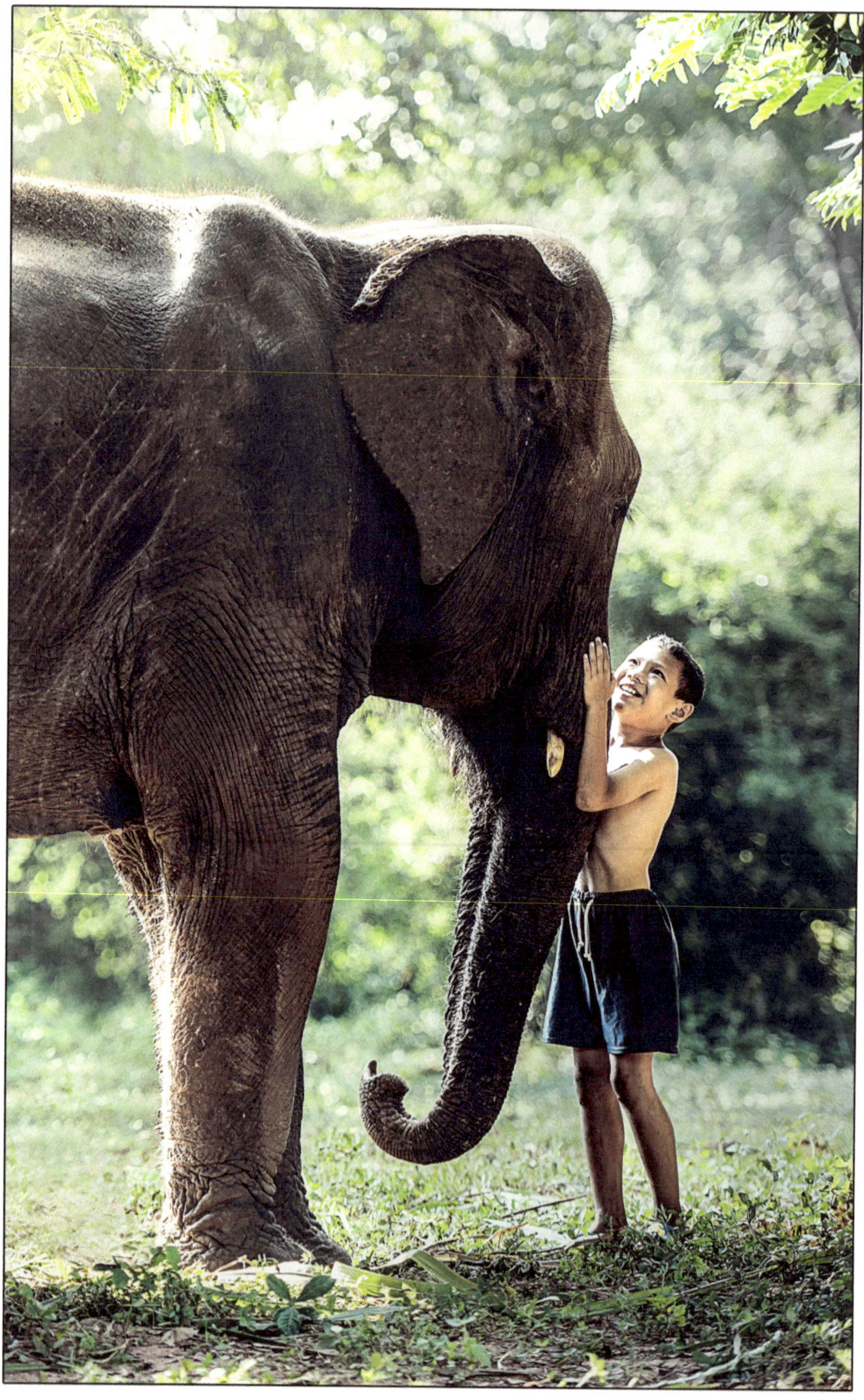

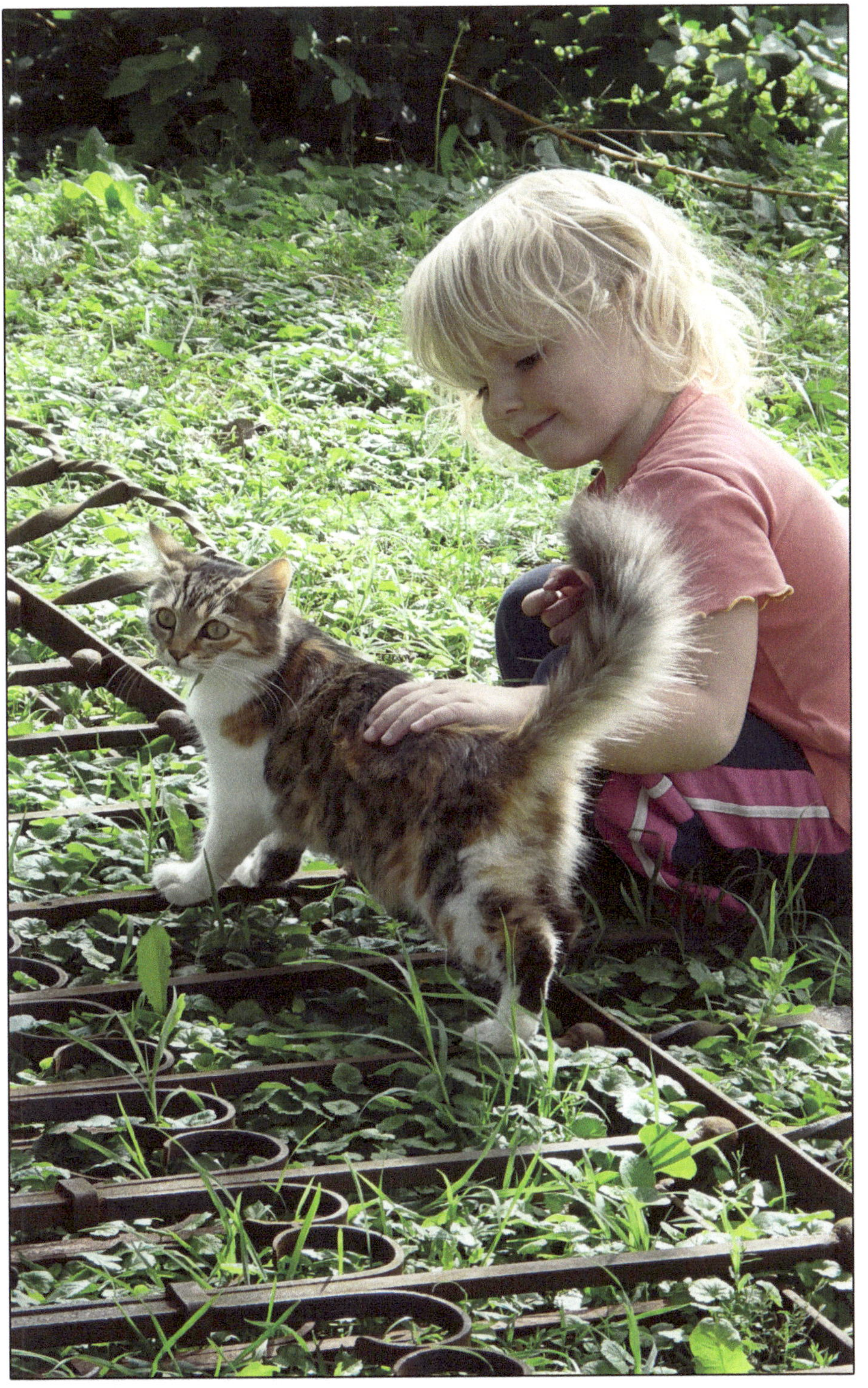

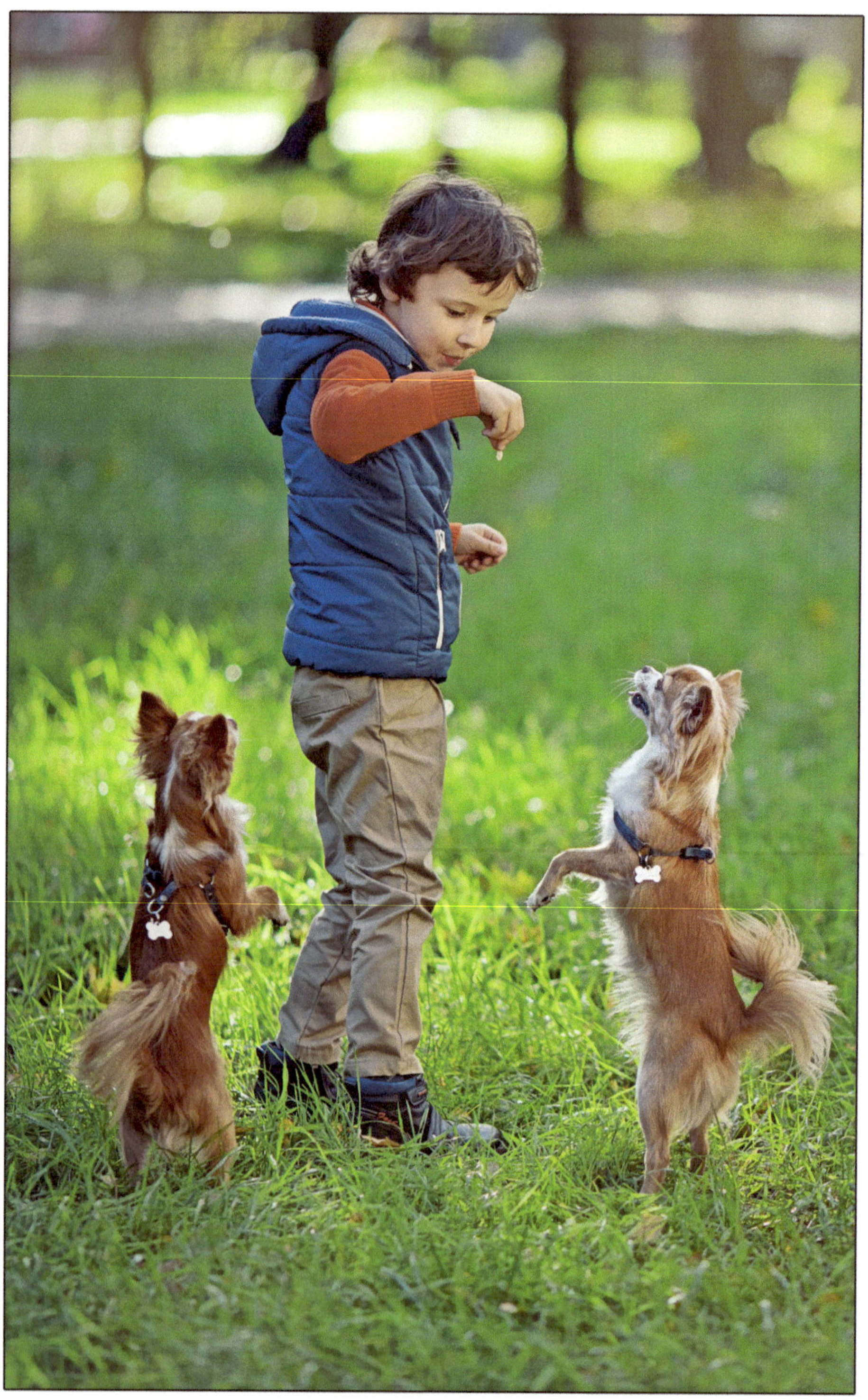

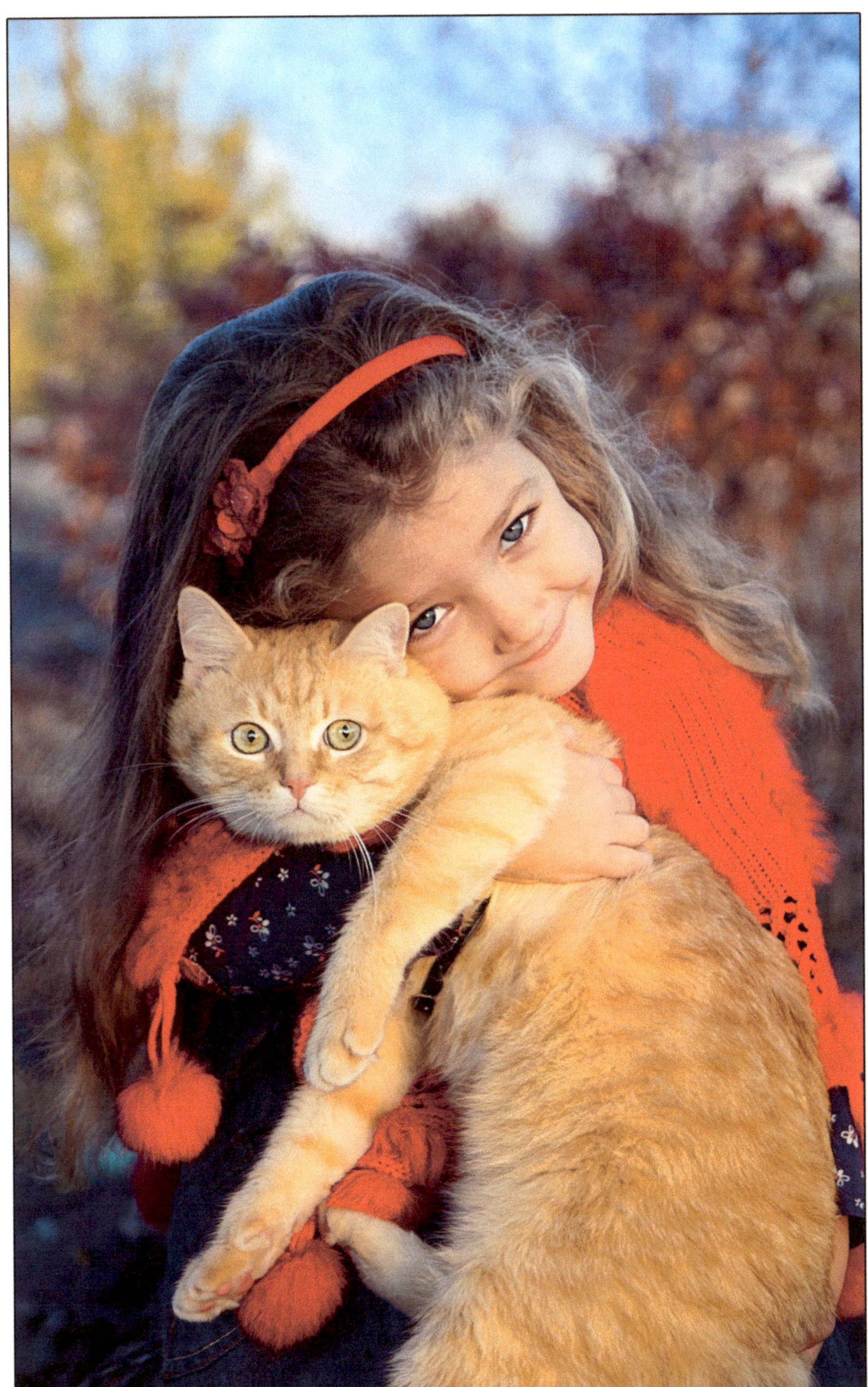

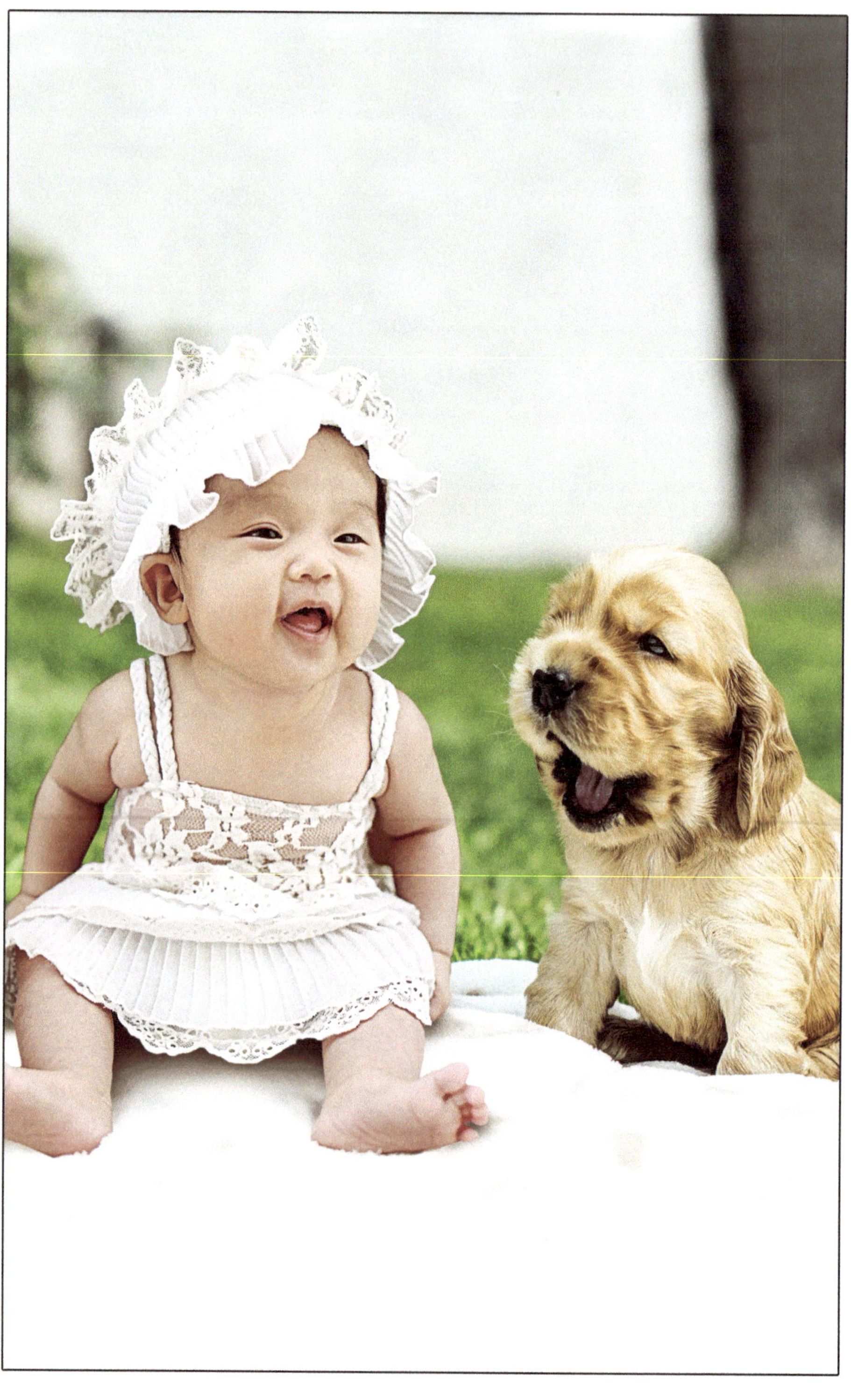

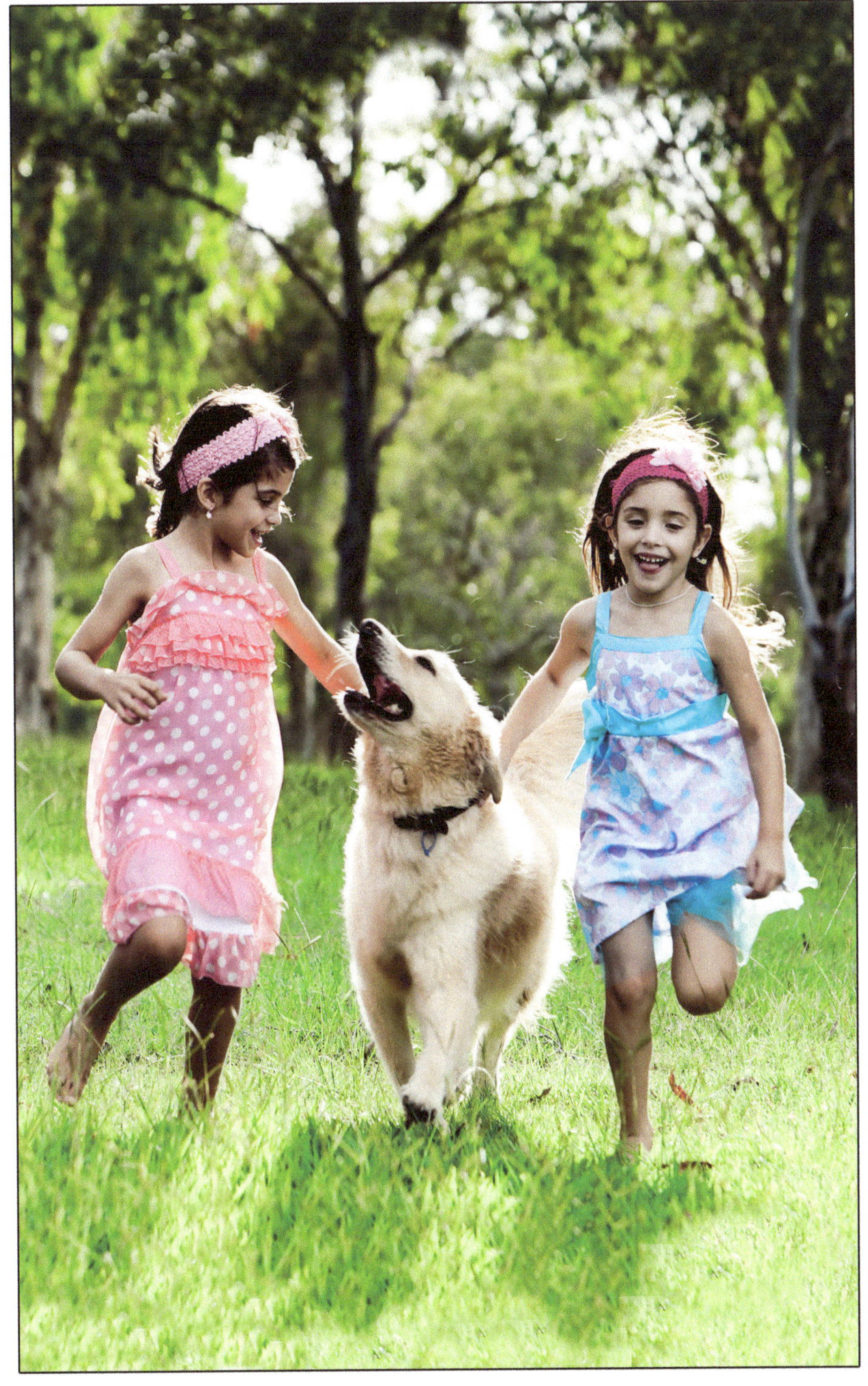

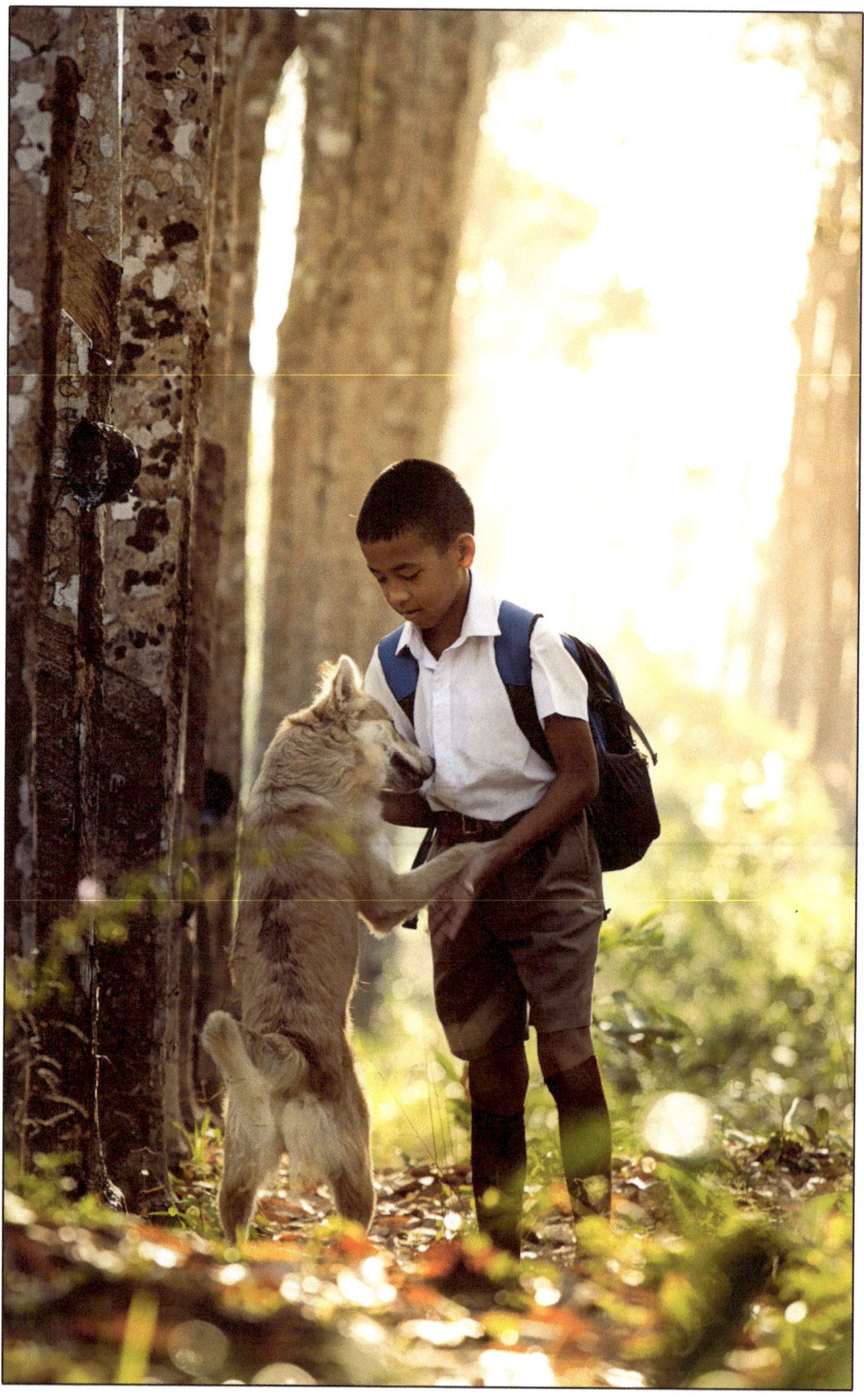

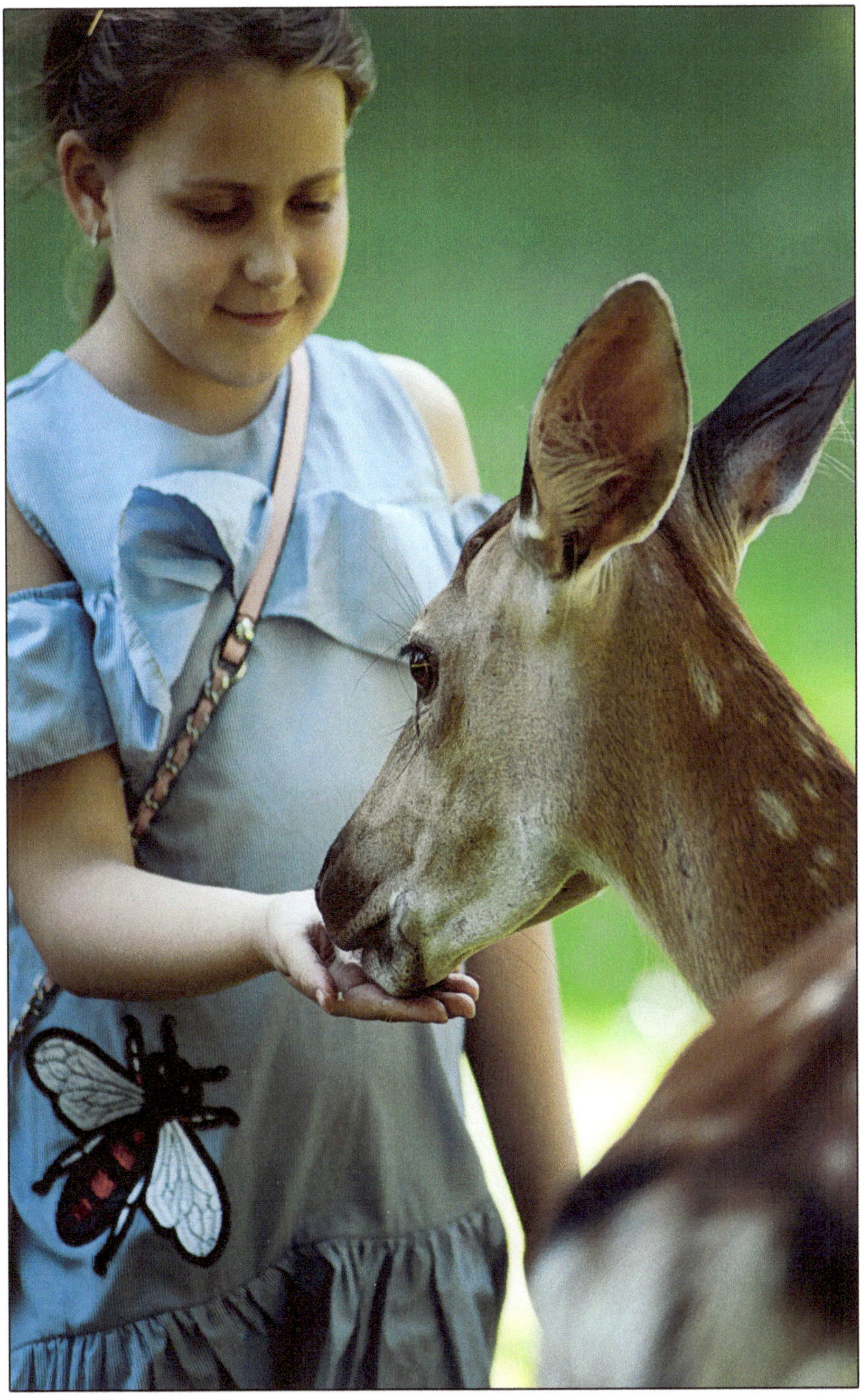

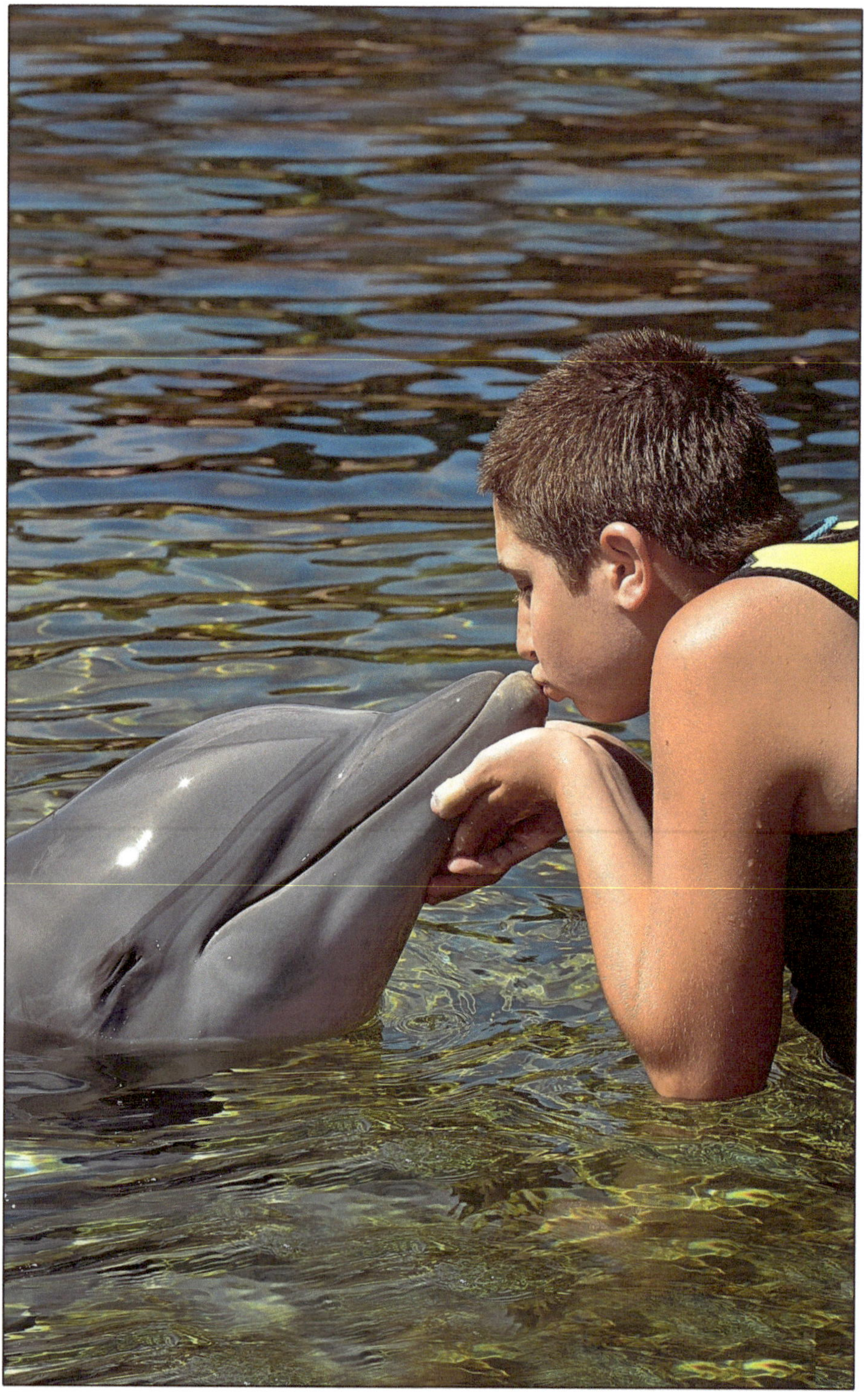

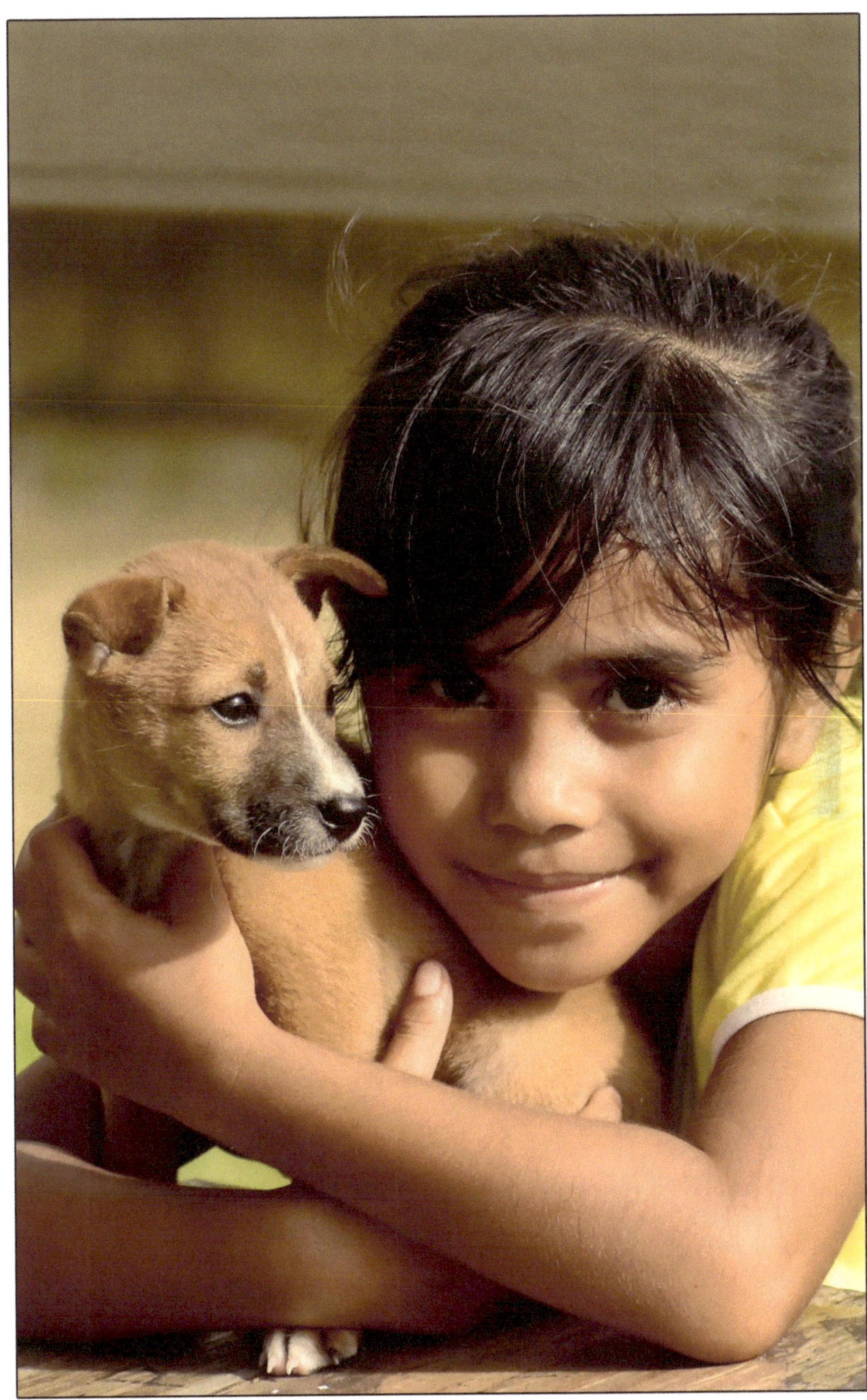

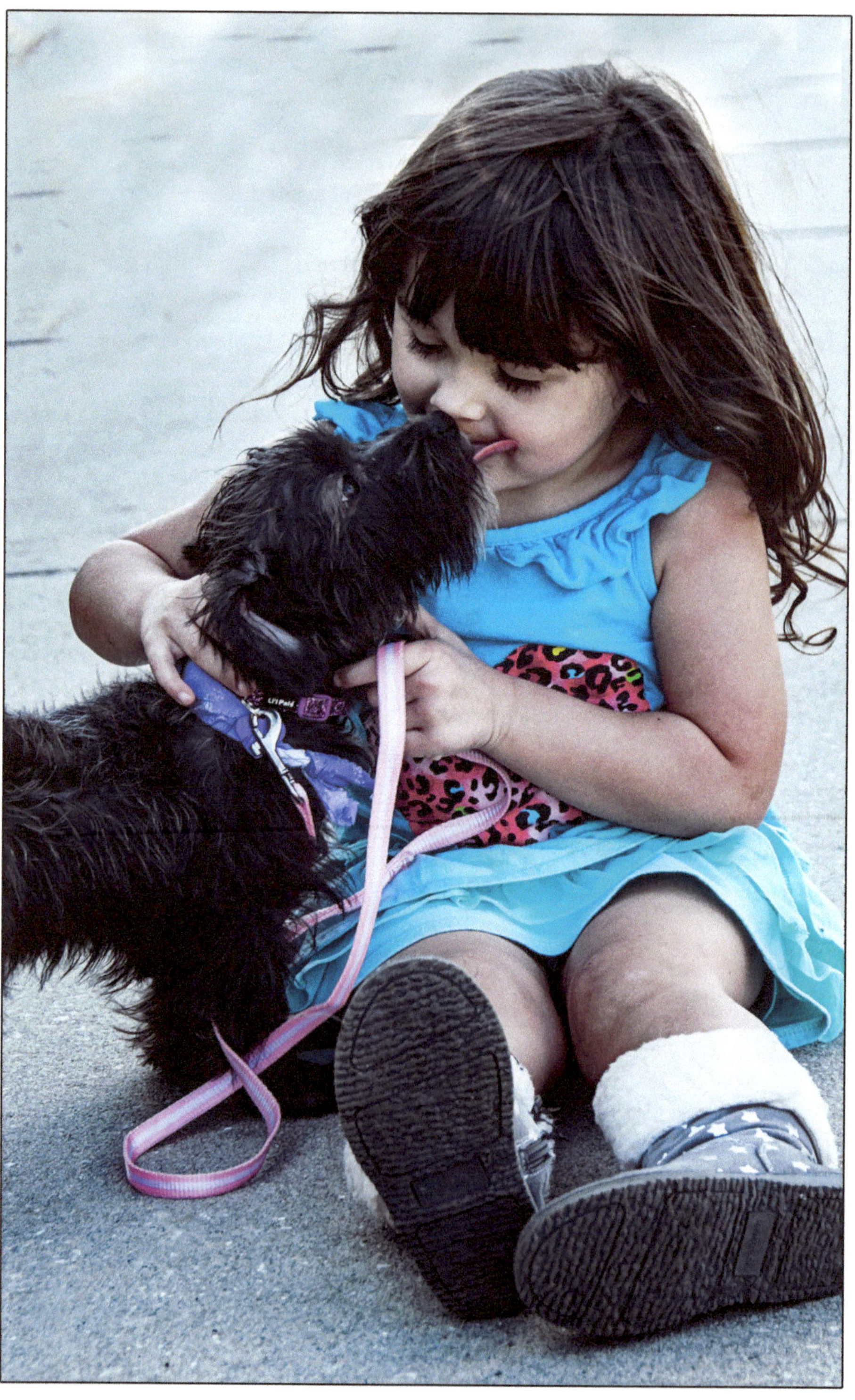

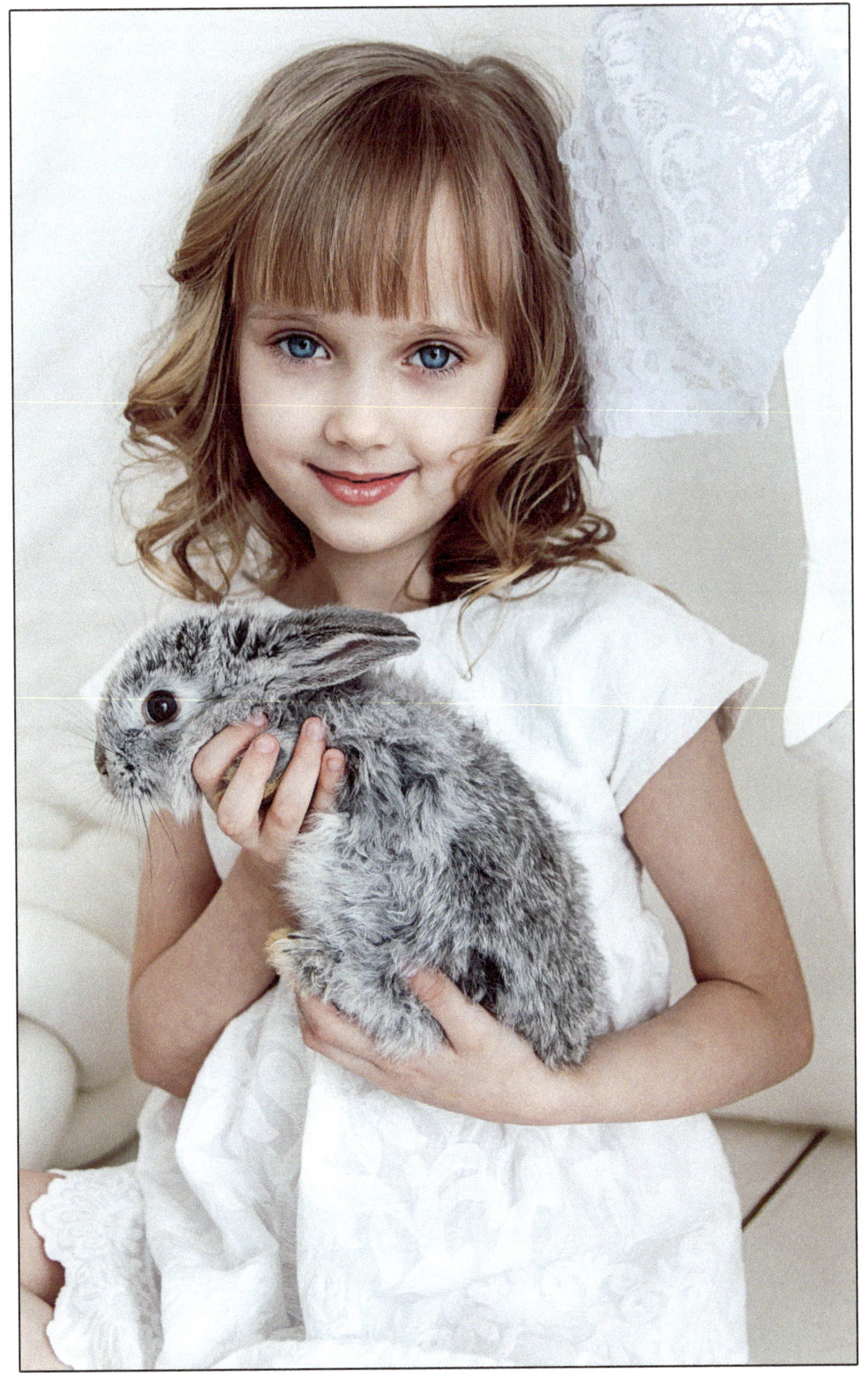

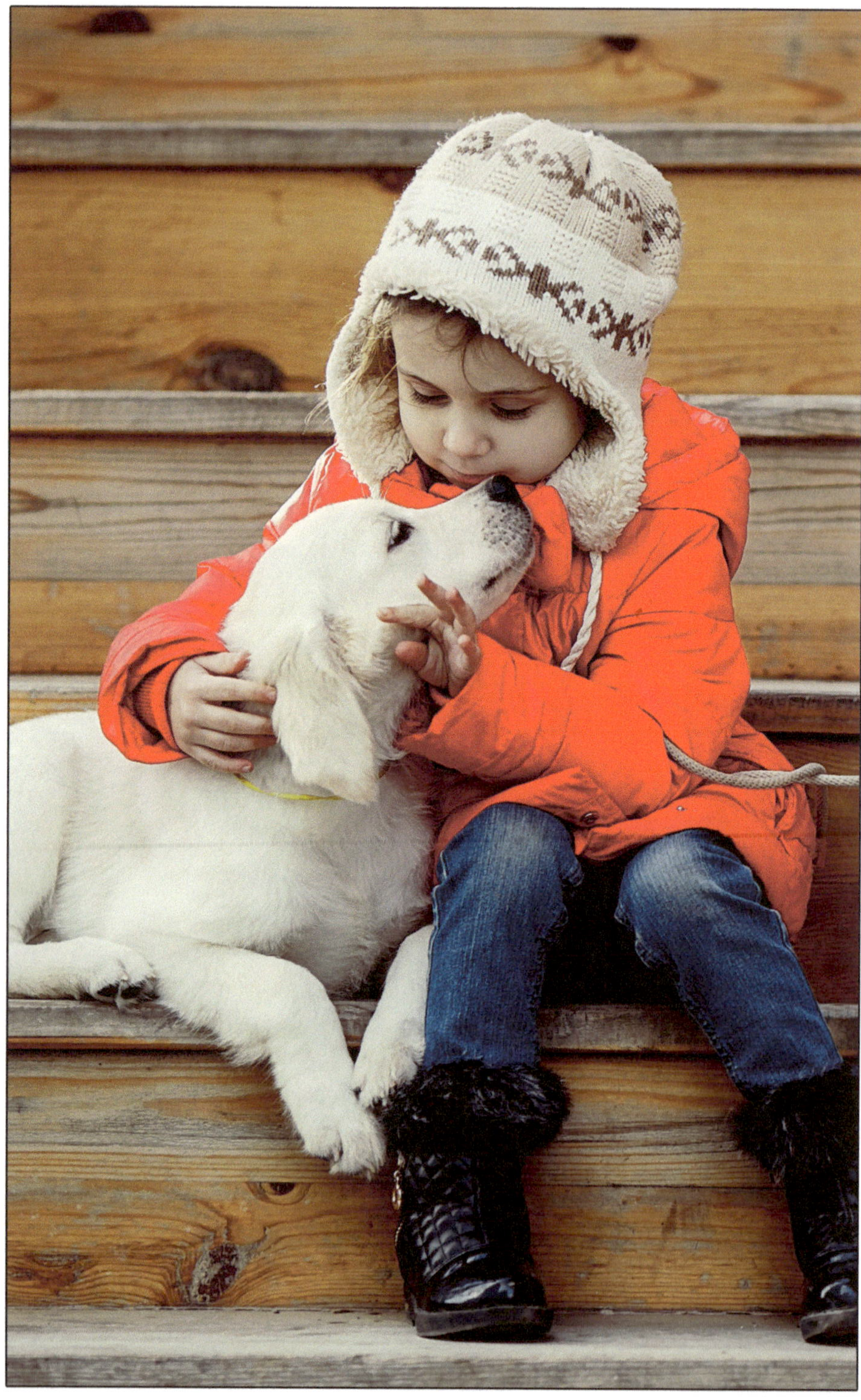

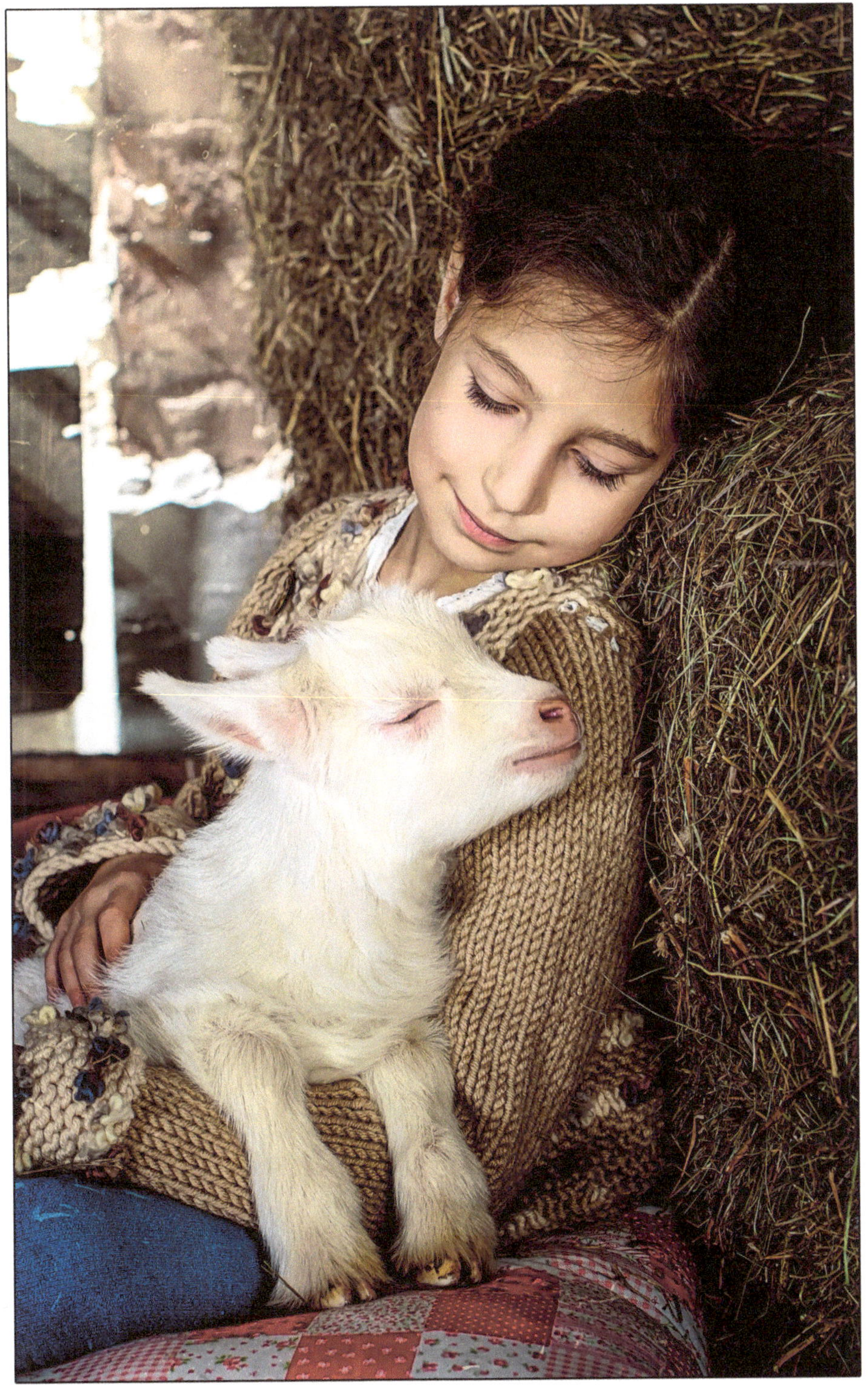

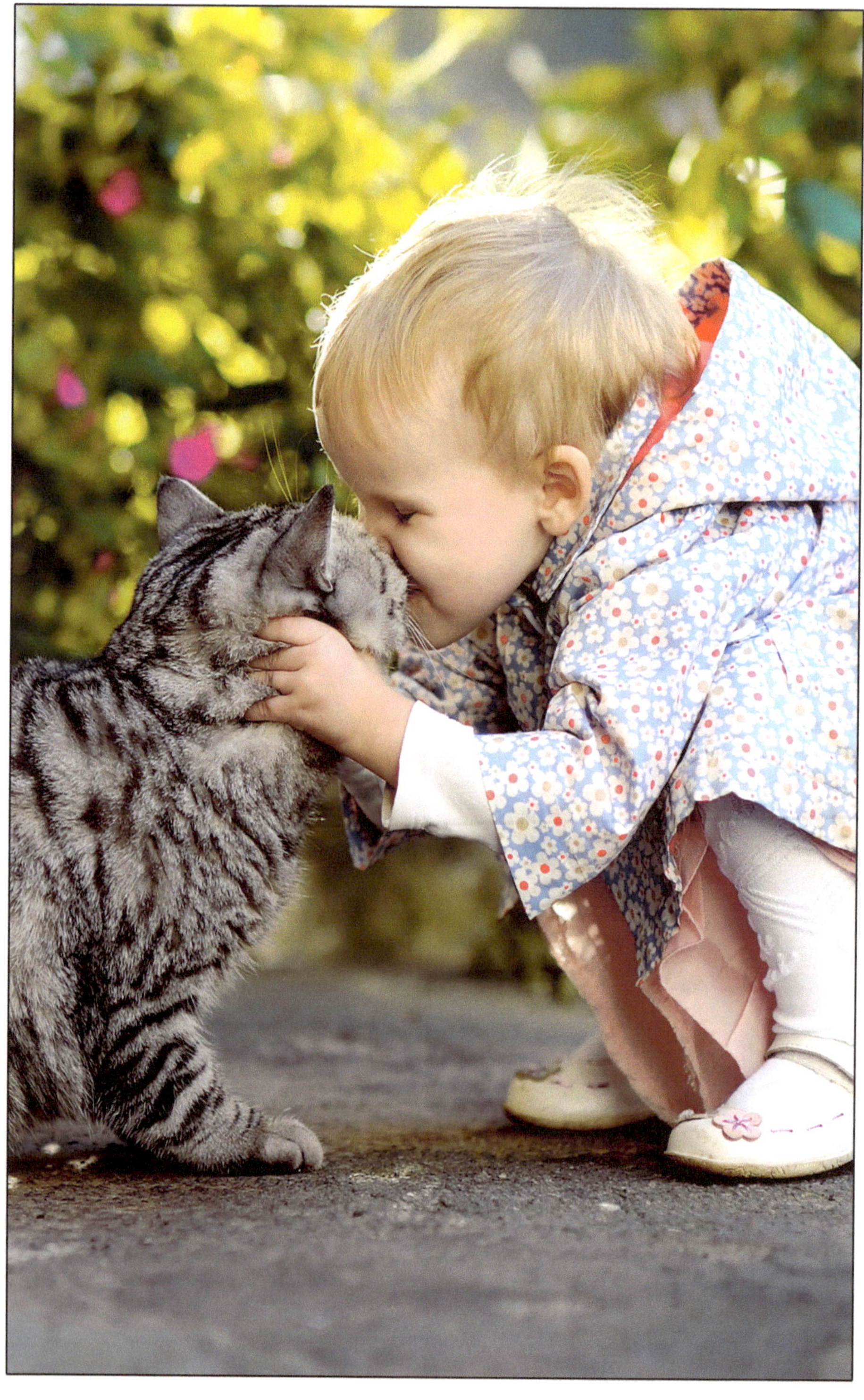

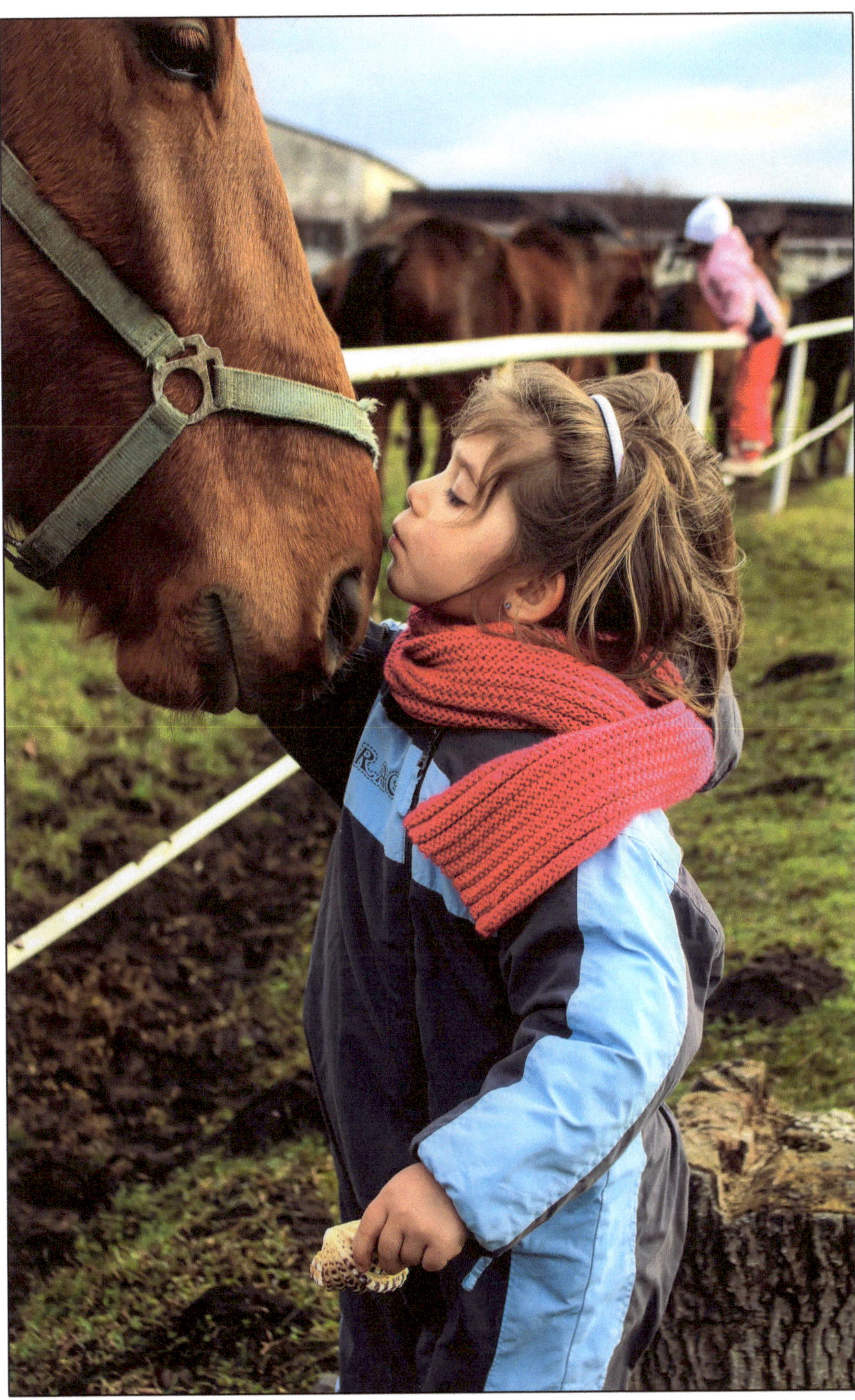

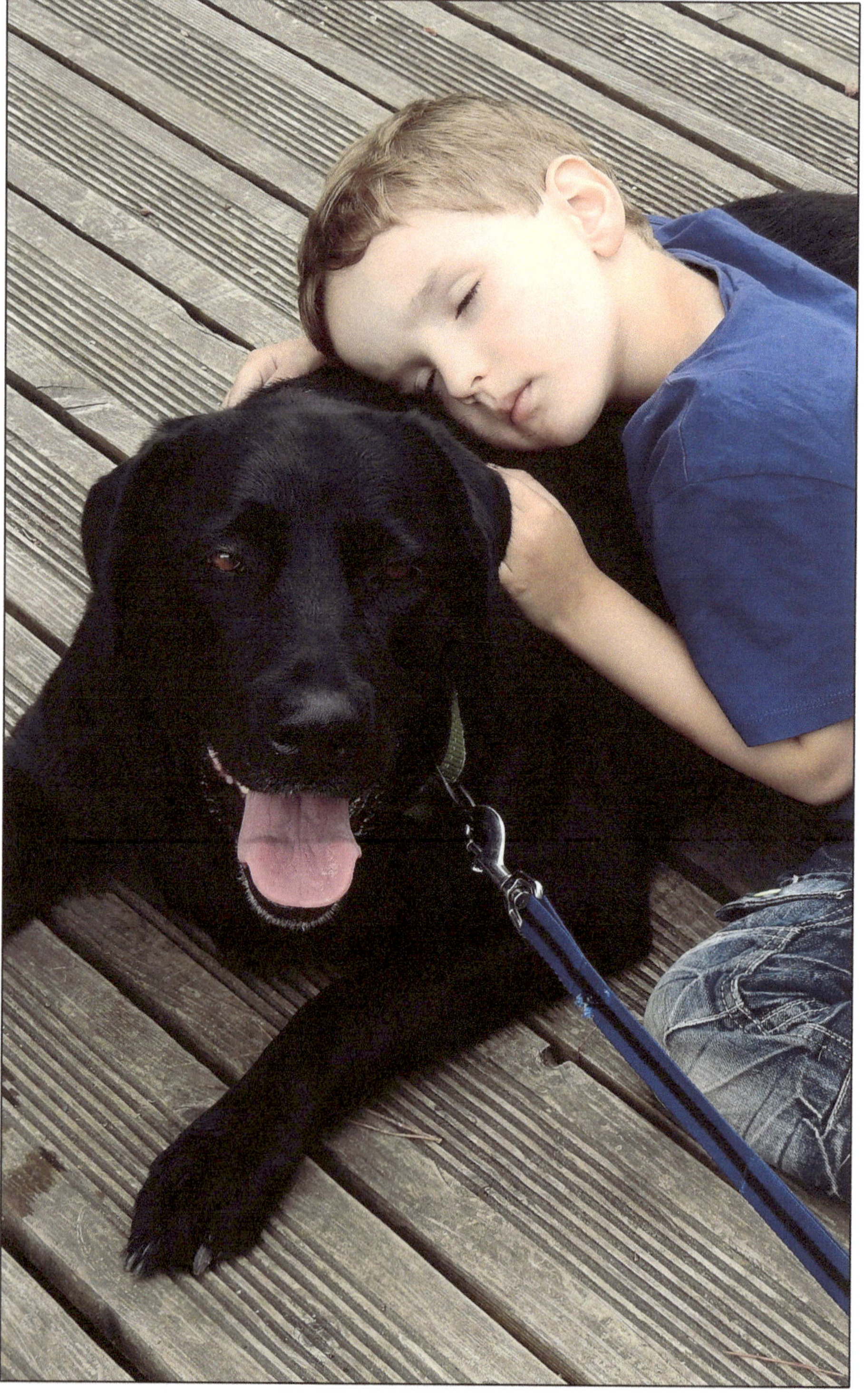

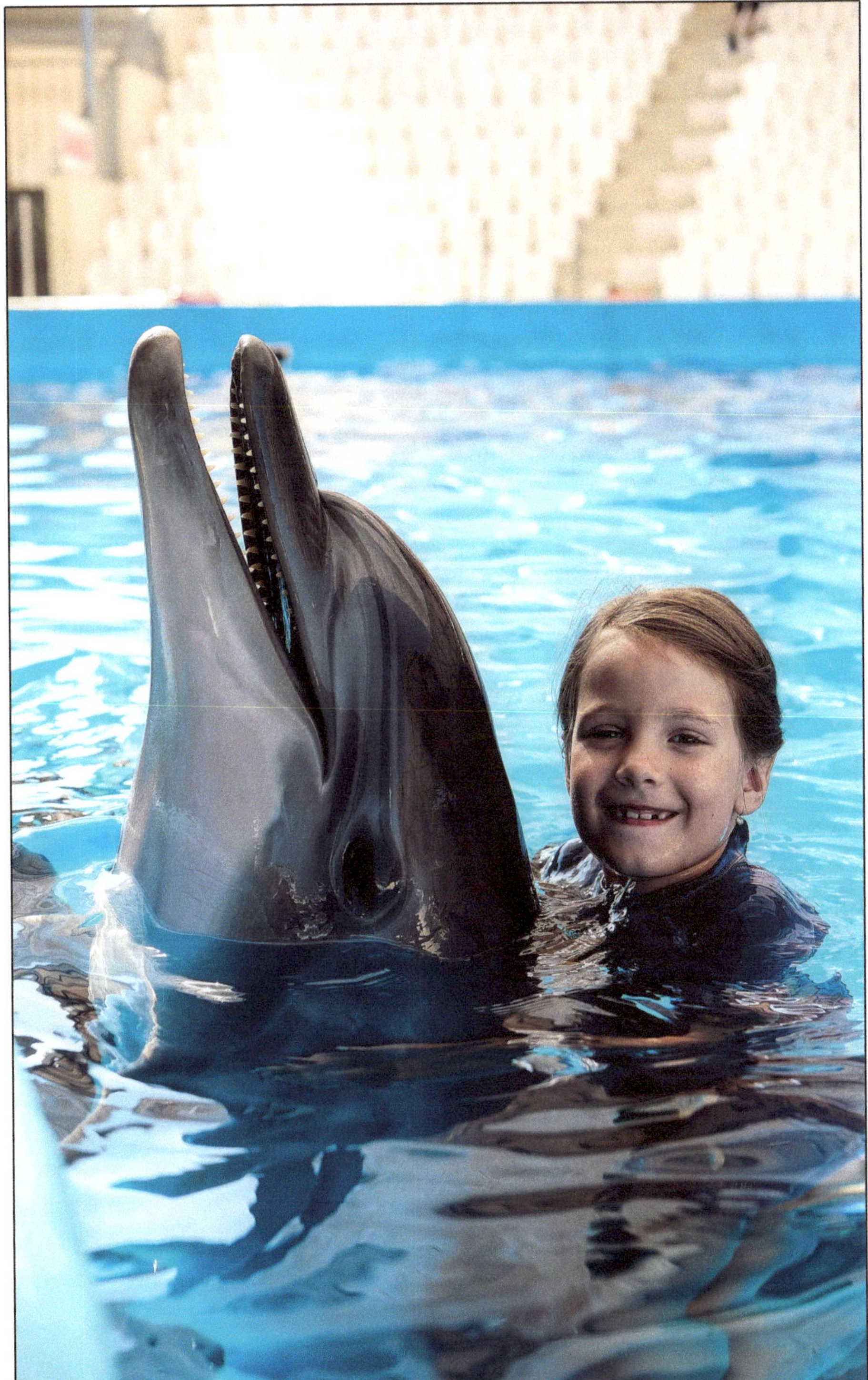

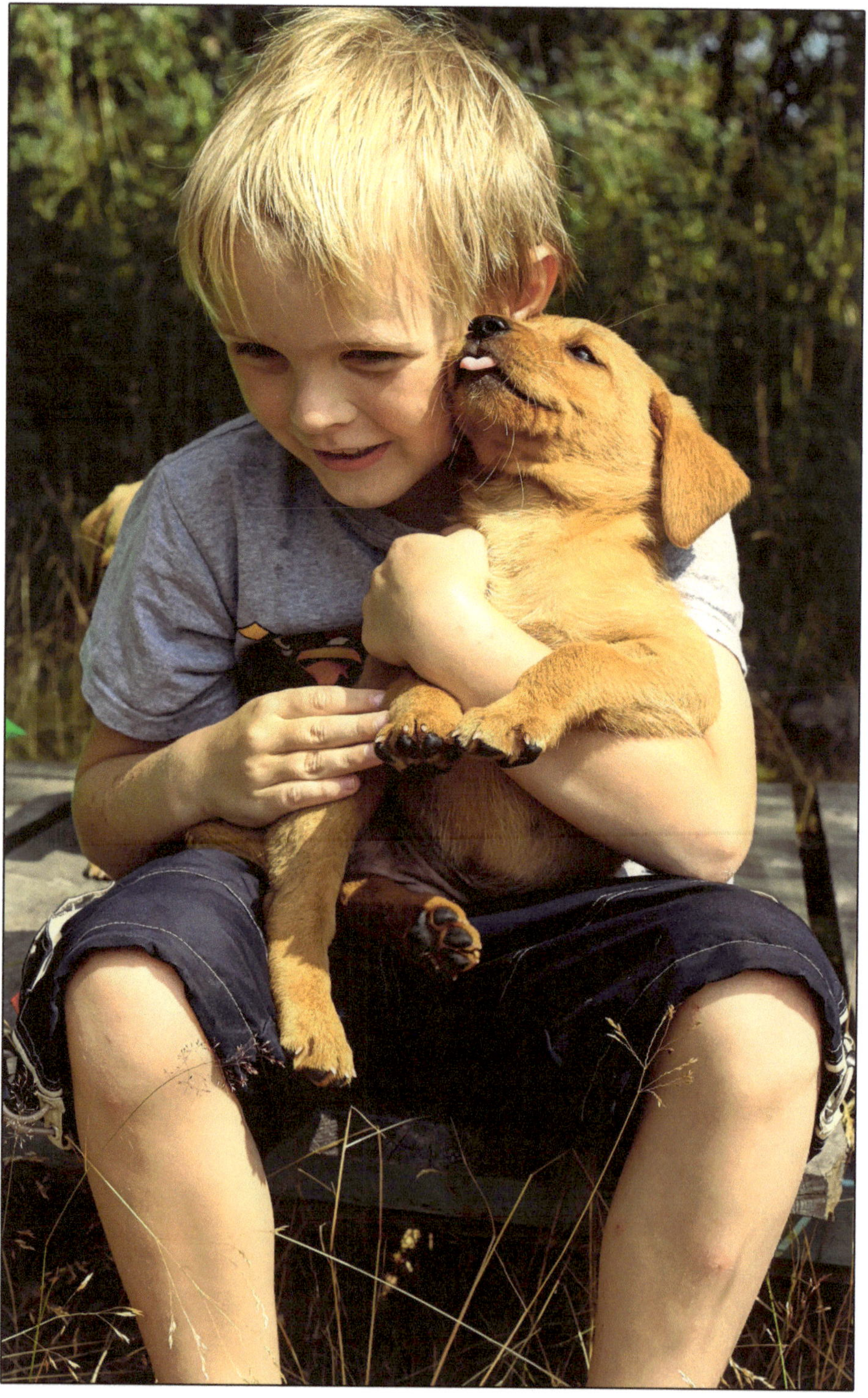

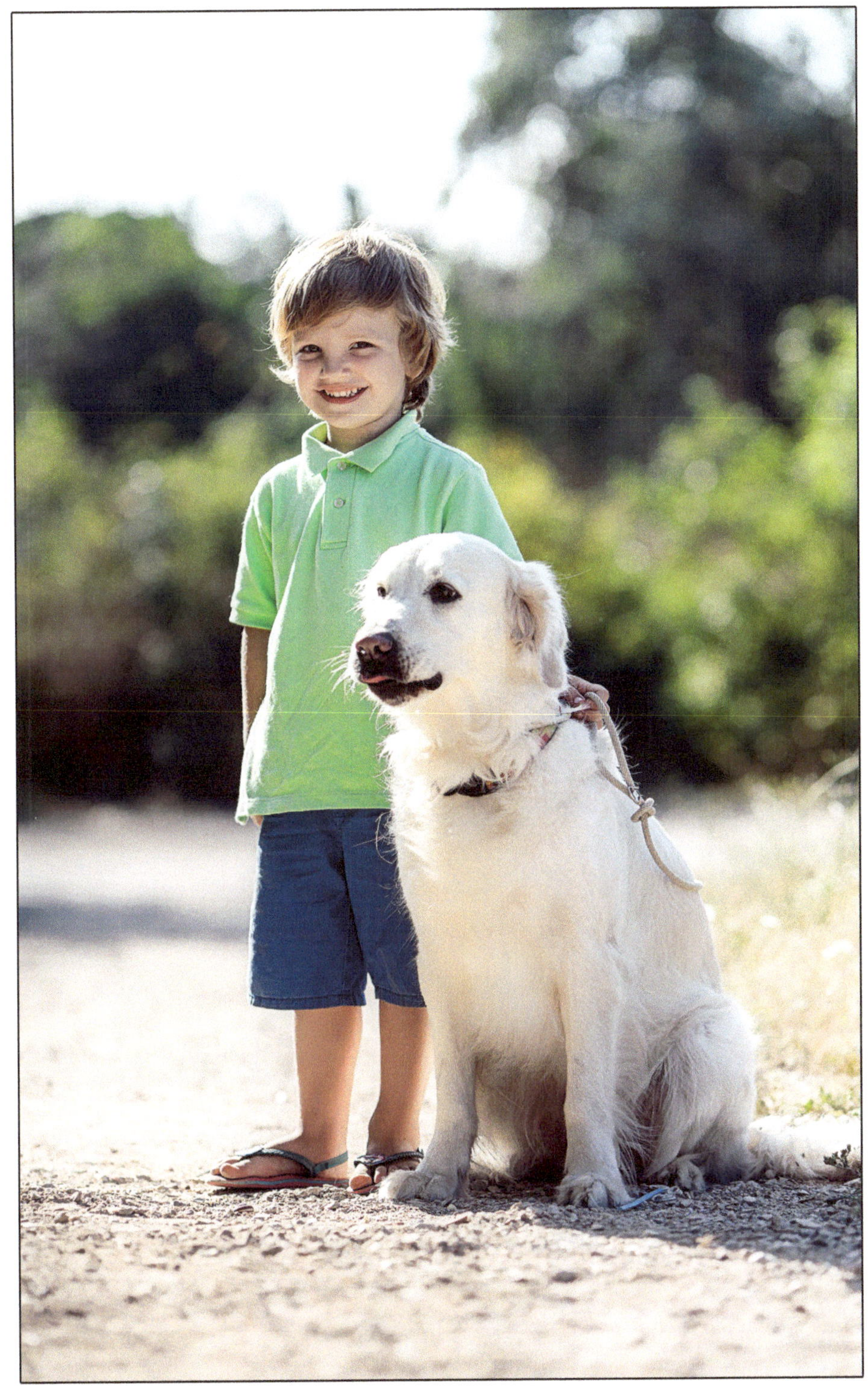

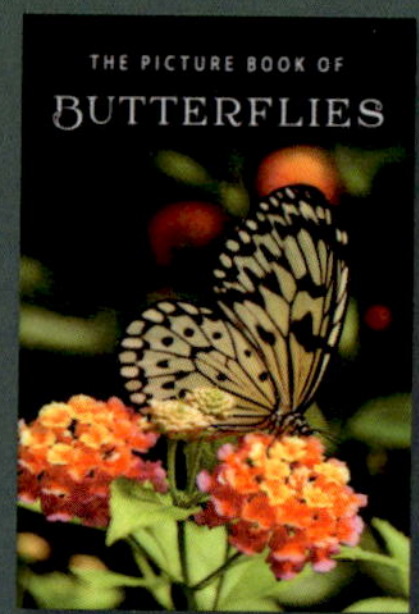

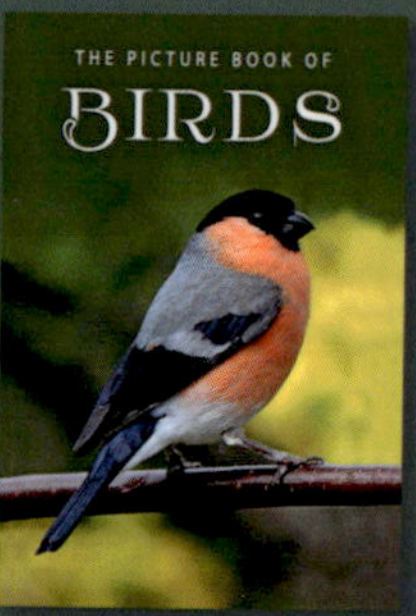

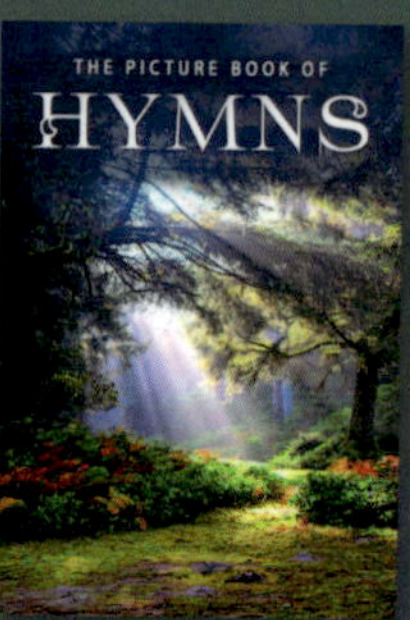

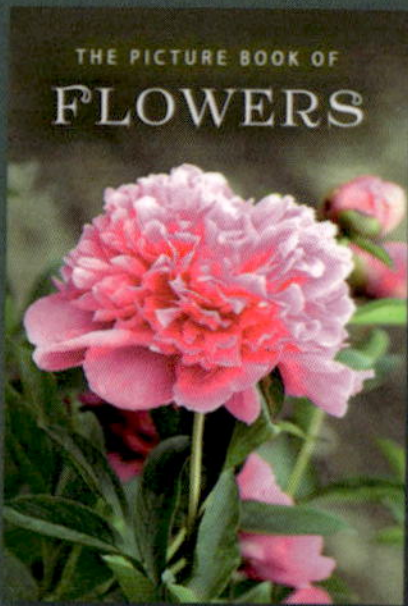

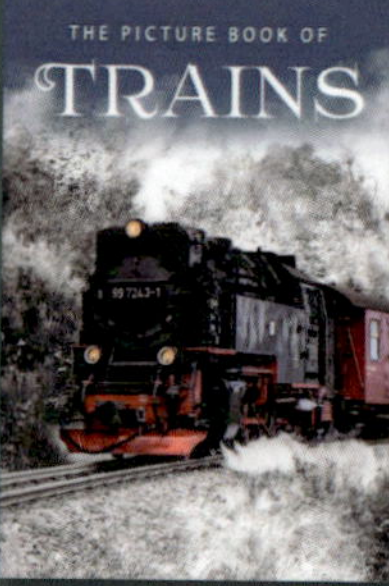

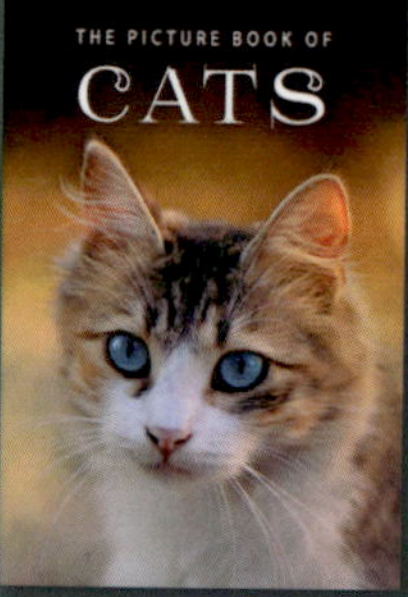

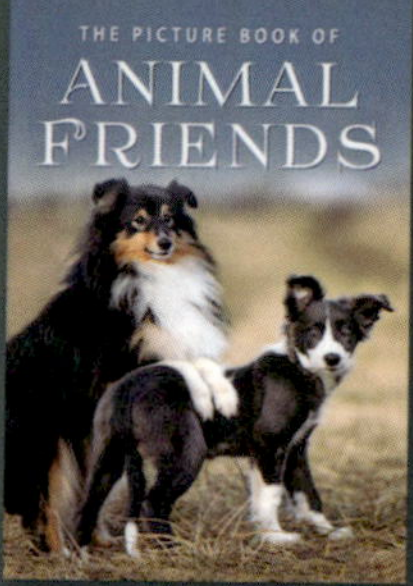

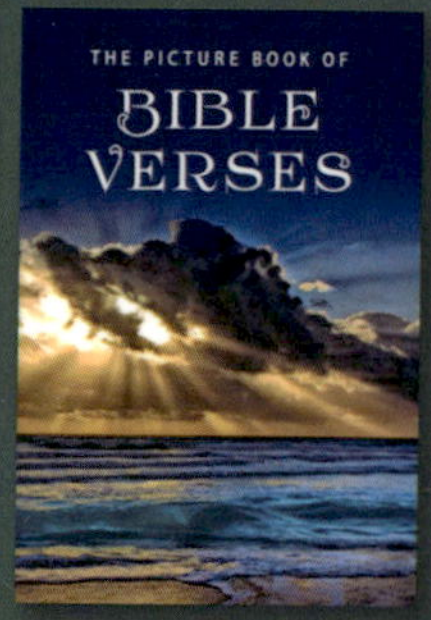

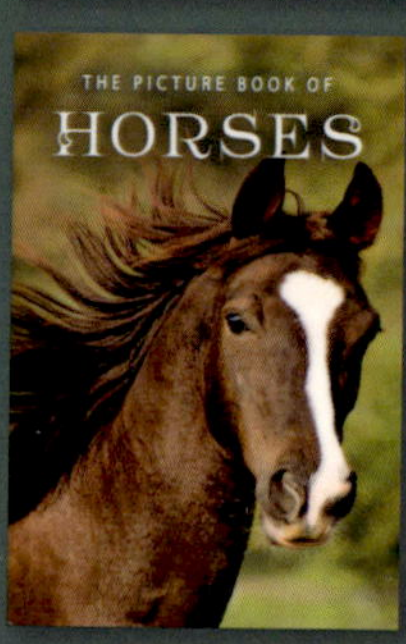

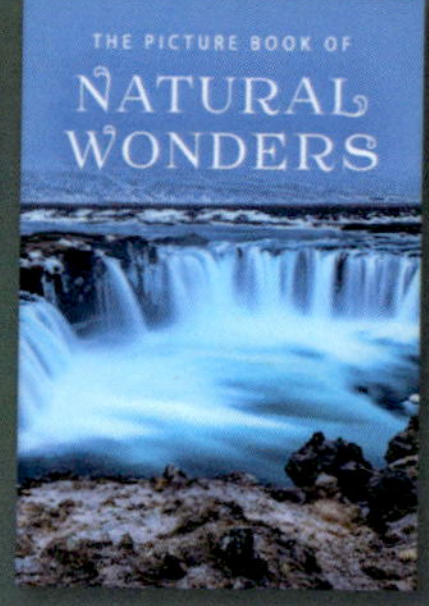

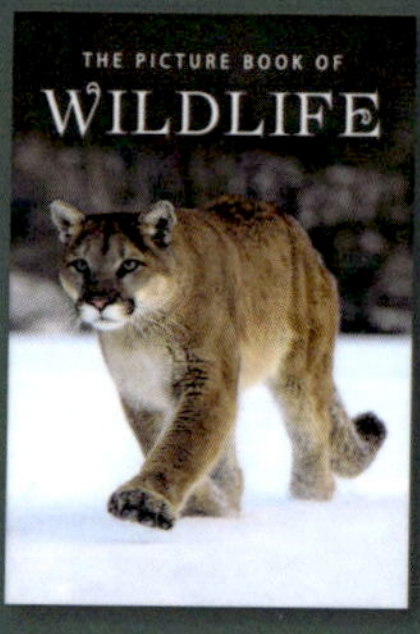

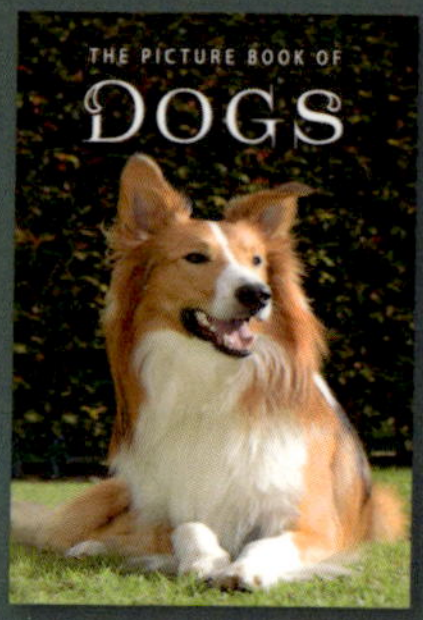

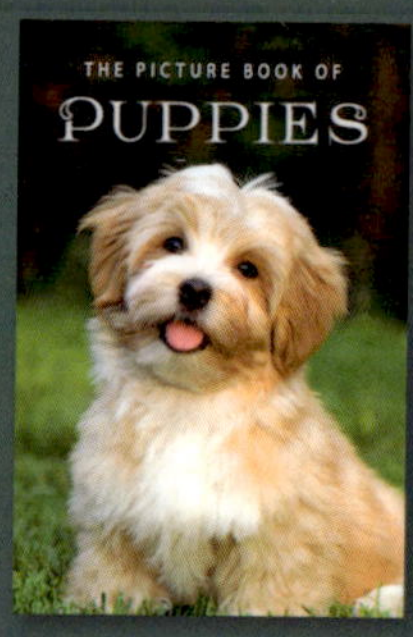

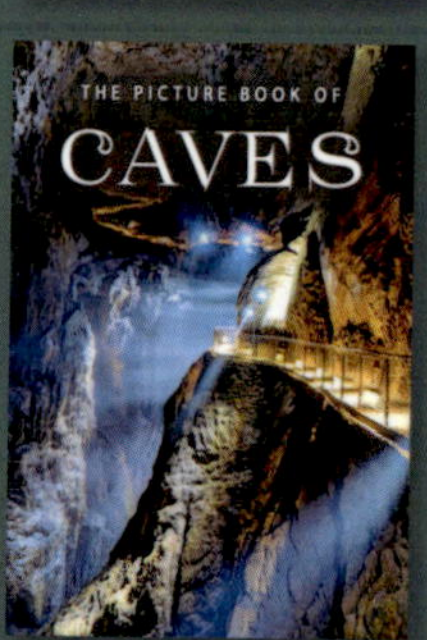

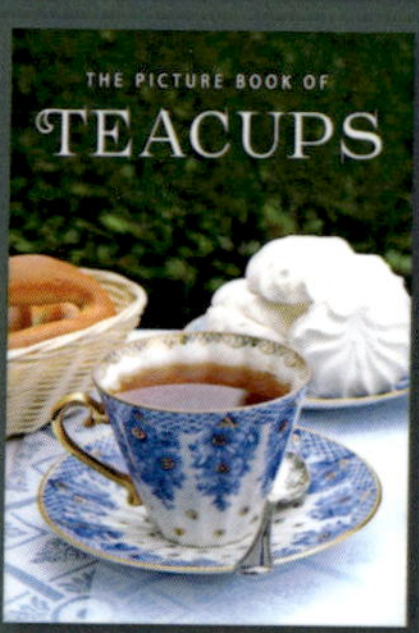

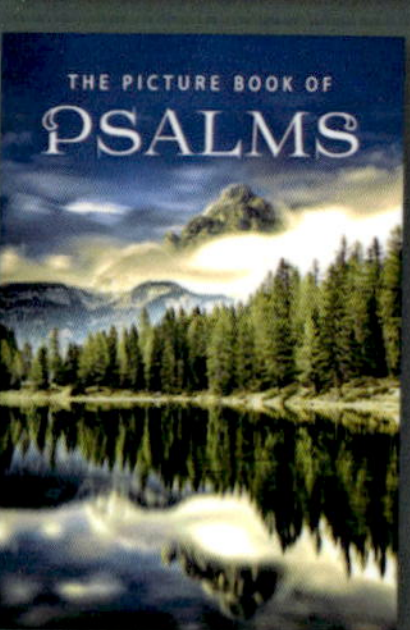

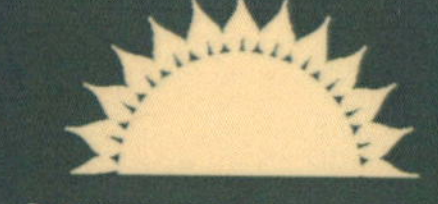

SUNNY STREET
BOOKS

SunnyStreetBooks.com

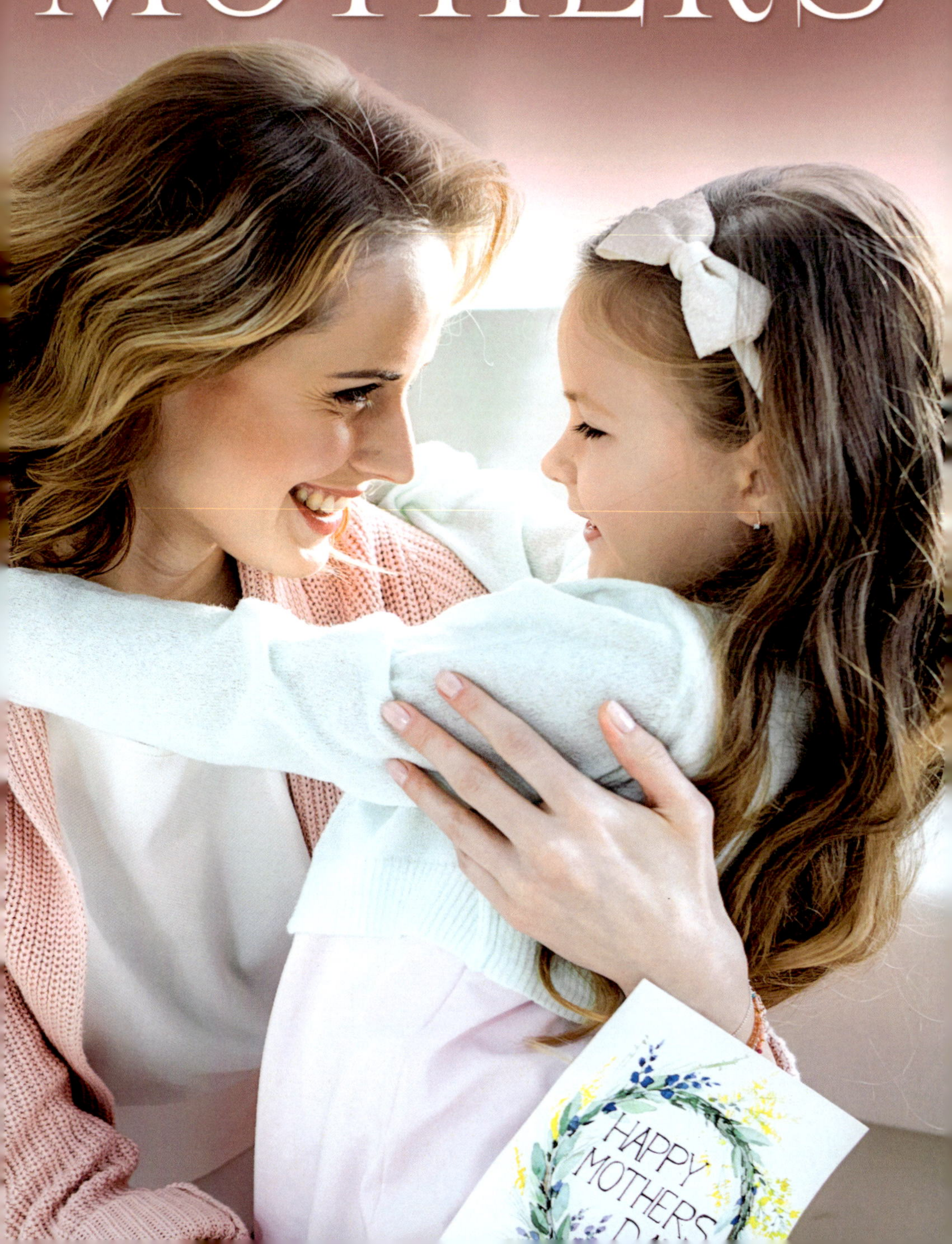
THE PICTURE BOOK OF
MOTHERS
HAPPY MOTHERS